Just Listen 'n Learn

French • Spanish • German
Italian • Japanese
Russian • Arabic • Greek

TEACHER'S MANUAL

Daniel Rolfs, Ph.D.

PASSPORT BOOKS
a division of *NTC Publishing Group*
Lincolnwood, Illinois USA

Also available:
Just Listen 'n Learn *Plus*:
Spanish, French, and German

Published by Passport Books, a division of NTC Publishing Group.
© 1994, 1985 by NTC Publishing Group, 4255 West Touhy Avenue,
Lincolnwood (Chicago), Illinois 60646-1975 U.S.A.
All rights reserved. No part of this book may be reproduced, stored
in a retrieval system, or transmitted in any form or by any means,
electronic, mechanical, photocopying, recording or otherwise, without
the prior permission of NTC Publishing Group.
Manufactured in the United States of America.

3 4 5 6 7 8 9 0 ML 0 9 8 7 6 5 4 3 2 1

Contents

About the *Just Listen 'n Learn* Series   1

Suggestions for Using the Tape Recorder   3

Presenting the Material in the Classroom: Four Approaches   4
    Working through a Unit   4
    A Non-structured Approach   6
    Using the Tapes and Book as a Selected Grammar Review   9
    A Gradated Program for Developing Increasing Levels of Skill   10

Appendix I: A Description of the Dialogues by Content   18

Appendix II: A Description of the Grammar Presented by Unit and Listing of Grammatical Exercises   42

Appendix III: A Catalogue and Description of the Comprehension Exercises According to Level of Skill Involved   63

Acknowledgment

Some of the ideas for use suggested in this Manual were based on strategies developed by Brian Hill, General Editor of the *Just Listen 'n Learn* Language Programs.

About the *Just Listen 'n Learn* Series

The *Just Listen 'n Learn* Language Programs were created from the refreshingly innovative ideal of selecting a number of predetermined topics and sending interviewers into the field with the purpose of recording spontaneous conversations with native speakers. The result of this effort is a generally parallel learning program in eight major languages: French, German, Italian, Spanish, Japanese, Russian, Greek, and Arabic.* Although originally intended for independent study, the programs can also serve quite well as a complete course or as a supplement in a classroom. Ideally, it should be adopted between the second- and fourth-year level of high school, at an earlier level of a college course, or as the basic program in adult/continuing education classes.

The purpose of this Manual is to suggest four general ways in which the program can be implemented in the classroom setting. However, it should be stressed that the ideas that follow are provided primarily as a *guide*, and that you should be flexible and imaginative in incorporating the tapes and written material into a broader curriculum. In short, the material is so varied and rich in potential that you will soon have many ideas of your own, which you should feel free to try.

At the very least, *Just Listen 'n Learn* can be of considerable value to the classroom simply as a means of creating greater *interest* in a foreign language as a result of presenting it, through the taped dialogues, in a lively and highly relevant form. Beyond this, the program also offers students a notable psychological benefit, in that working with tapes of this nature will help many to overcome the common obstacles of self-consciousness and timidity which they might otherwise contend with when leaving the classroom and traveling in a foreign land. In the process of overcoming these obstacles, the student of course will become far more able to develop that sense of authentic self-confidence which is crucial to attaining fluency.

Certainly the taped materials in the *Just Listen 'n Learn* series provide an accurate simulation of much of the linguistic experience of traveling in another

---

* Examples in the introductory material are taken from the French, German, Italian, and Spanish programs. Nonetheless, the Japanese, Russian, Greek, and Arabic programs follow the same format.

country. In contrast to the typical classroom situation, in which the main voice heard is that of a single person (the teacher)—and even in contrast to many traditional language laboratory programs, in which one hears the same voices of a limited number of actors reading from scripts—the dialogues in *Just Listen 'n Learn* include a wide variety of speakers with many different vocal pitches, inflections, and regional accents, who represent differing levels of education and speak on a broad spectrum of topics in natural situations. On some of the tapes, such as those made at airports and in railroad stations, there is even the dimension of authentic "background" sounds which recreate the listening environment often found while traveling. All of this will help students develop an ear for the language as it is spoken in day-to-day life.

In addition, the tapes of course provide a learning content that will prove more than useful to anyone who travels abroad. Besides dealing with practical problems such as ordering a meal at a restaurant, checking into a hotel, or buying a train ticket, the tapes also concentrate on the vital matter of "small talk," which is so important in meeting people and making friends—such as introducing oneself, speaking of one's hometown and family, or talking about that favorite subject of casual encounters, the weather.

One final advantage to the program should be pointed out with regard to the teacher. Since *Just Listen 'n Learn* is organized in a parallel format for all languages in the series, the teacher of more than one of these languages can easily transfer the techniques from one course to another. Similarly, different teachers using the program for different languages can readily compare notes and share suggestions with one another, thereby enhancing their efforts in the classroom through a meaningful level of communication on curriculum.

Suggestions for Using the Tape Recorder

Before turning to a discussion of implementing the material in your course, you may wish to review these general observations on how best to use a cassette recorder (or cassette tape player) in the classroom:

1. Always store the cassettes in the container provided, as this will keep them free from harmful dust.

2. Do not store the cassettes near any magnetic sources (such as loudspeakers, amplifiers, or electric cables), or sources of heat (such as leaving them near a radiator, or in the sun), or in cold, dark places. Doing so may distort the quality of the tapes.

3. Using a cleaner, keep the recorder heads free of dust, since dirt on the heads can cause muffled sounds.

4. When playing tapes, it is usually best to place the tone setting away from *bass*, so as to avoid a "deep" and "mellow" sound, which can make words harder to understand. Instead, place the setting on *treble*, which produces an optimal "clear" and "crisp" sound.

5. If your class is small, you will not need a separate speaker. In fact, the students can sit in a circle or semi-circle *around* the tape recorder, which provides for good acoustics, and creates a friendly, relaxed atmosphere. If you have a large class, a loudspeaker may help. Ideally, there should be one or more *extension* speakers, which you can place in the best possible position(s). Before playing the tape for the class, experiment in an empty classroom by walking around, to make sure the tape can be heard equally well from every angle.

6. Although it is generally best not to interrupt the tape the first time it is played, on subsequent playings it may be helpful to make judicious use of the "pause" button in order to answer questions, allow time for writing, clarify grammatical points, and so on.

Presenting the Material in the Classroom: Four Approaches

The four approaches which follow begin with an opening discussion on using the tapes and book as a self-contained course, and continue with three further segments on how the program can be implemented as a supplement to a basic textbook you may already be using. Depending on a variety of factors (such as the level of your class, the past experience of your students with taped materials, or the nature of other materials employed in your course), you may find that one of these approaches works better than the others. It is equally possible that, after some experimentation, you may end up *combining* various aspects of each approach. In any case, feel free to experiment until you have discovered what seems to work best, and which activities produce the most positive feedback from your students.

Working through a Unit

If you are using *Just Listen 'n Learn* as the basic component of your course, you will probably prefer to follow the units in the order in which they are presented in the program, even though this is not absolutely necessary. It is possible, for example, depending on a teacher's individual style, to begin with a later unit in which the verbs used on the tapes are explained and drilled in the book, rather than an earlier unit in which the definite article is similarly emphasized. For those who intend to vary the order of the units, however, it is advisable to at least begin with the first few as numbered in the program, since, due to their subject matter (simple greetings and phrases of courtesy, etc.), they are of the least difficulty and consequently will provide a more relaxed and comfortable "opening" for the course. Thereafter, you may choose which unit to present next either according to the grammatical points you wish to teach (see Appendix II, "A Description of the Grammar Presented by Unit and Listing of Grammatical Exercises"), or according to the content of the dialogues themselves (see Appendix I, "A Description of the Dialogues by Content"). Whatever your preference as to the order in which you will present the units, you may find helpful the general procedures suggested below—at least for the first time through. Later you will probably want to streamline at least some parts of the process.

Procedure

1. Orient yourself to the material at hand by turning to the first page of the unit. where you will find the following information:

    What You Will Learn
    These comments provide a description of the practical usefulness of the

content of the dialogues (e.g., "how to greet people," "how to say where you are from," "observing basic courtesies," etc.)

Study Guide
These notes show how best to group the dialogues you will play, in terms of their subject matter, length, and the difficulty of absorbing the material presented. On the basis of the guidelines, you may find it convenient to draw brackets around the groupings of dialogues in your book.

Before You Begin
This section identifies grammatical material to be reviewed from the previous unit. (It will be relevant, of course, only if you are working through units in succession.)

2. Draw up a list of the vocabulary items that will be necessary for working with the dialogues. This can be done in three ways: by reading the dialogues and keeping in mind the level of your class; by referring to the segments at the bottom of each dialogue in which difficult passages or unfamiliar vocabulary items are translated; and by consulting the *Key Words and Phrases* section, which follows the presentation of the dialogues as a whole.

3. Before playing a given tape, orient the class. Having the students keep their books closed, describe the contents of the tape, review vocabulary (putting important items on the board), and explain any grammar points you feel need special attention. It is particularly important, at least in the beginning, to try to minimize possible discouragement on the part of your students by pointing out that this may be a relatively new experience for many, and that they should not worry too much if they don't understand everything the first time, since you will replay the tape. Stress that building oral comprehension skills takes time and patience but can be very rewarding.

4. With all books closed, play the dialogues according to the groupings suggested. Then replay them, making judicious use of the "pause" button in order to answer questions, comment, or explain. Then replay the dialogues without interruption. Finally, replay the dialogues with the students' following along in the book.

5. Continue on to supplementary material. Each unit contains five types of supplementary material, which you may approach in any order and work through in whole or only in part. Here is a description of each, with a few comments:

Practice What You Have Learned
This section consists of exercises in the book, based on the tape just played. Some exercises require the student to write in the book while the tape is replayed; others are done in silence. Most of these exercises can be done in the classroom.

Your Turn to Speak
This section consists of *oral* exercises done in conjunction with the tape and

requires the student to speak as prompted by the "guide." Many of these exercises can be done in the classroom with you, the teacher, participating. (This, in fact, would be ideal, since in the beginning you can serve as an important model to give your students courage.) Note that this sort of group activity is possible only when the tape requires specific, predictable answers, such as when the guide prompts, "Say you are from the United States," and the class does so by repeating a phrase it has just heard on the tape. Other exercises, however, are more open-ended in the responses required, such as when the guide, recreating a scene in a café, says, "Now order something to drink." Since, clearly, the latter type of exercise cannot be done chorally, it is very important that you screen the contents of the *Your Turn to Speak* segment of the tape *before* introducing it in the classroom.

Grammar
This section consists of written exercises illustrating constructions presented in the dialogue but done *without* the tape. (A typical exercise, for example, might consist of filling in blanks in sentences with the correct form of the definite article, verbs, or adjectives.) This material can be done in class but might better be assigned as homework, especially in conjunction with other material covered in a standard grammar textbook.

Read and Understand
Also done without tapes, this section of each unit consists of interpreting written material (such as signs, maps, menus, train schedules, and so on), and usually has accompanying questions at the bottom of the page. This material can also be covered in class—perhaps in the form of a discussion—or assigned as homework.

Did You Know?
Here you will find often highly interesting segments, written in English, offering cultural background on a wide variety of subjects, such as leisure activities preferred by the French (p. 199); changing fashions in German first names (p. 19); Italian driving habits (p. 173); or certain peculiarities of Spanish table manners (p. 145). These segments have no exercises, but at least occasionally you may wish to discuss them in class or assign them to be read at home.

A Non-structured Approach

Turning now to the methods by means of which *Just Listen 'n Learn* can be implemented as *supplementary* material, let us first consider a relatively "non-structured" approach. Certainly the program can be employed in an improvisational way, i.e., not as "work" to be completed in the classroom, but rather as the basis for communicative activities. Viewed in this light, the written dialogues and accompanying tapes can be treated as a purely supplementary activity which can stimulate interest and provide a new dimension of linguistic experience for the class. Although you may wish to try some of the activities discussed in this section, quite possibly your main use of the tapes will be simply to play them and enjoy them with the class, for additional listening comprehension and variety, after a session of concentrated effort on something else.

The Selection of Tapes

If you decide to use the program in this way, you may wonder which tapes would be most useful and most enjoyed, so a few remarks on that subject may prove helpful. Since the subject matter of the dialogues in the very beginning of each book is generally the least complex, you will probably want to begin with the initial units. Thereafter, however, you will find that there is not a great deal of difference in the level of difficulty of subsequent units, so you should feel free to skip around and choose on the basis of what you feel would be most interesting.

In selecting material, you can of course refer to the table of contents, but there are several drawbacks to relying exclusively on the very general descriptions at the beginning of the book. Sometimes there is much more variety in the dialogues than indicated by the title heading; sometimes dialogues are included that are not obvious from the title; and furthermore, there is frequently some overlap of subject matter from unit to unit. For example, note that in several editions the dialogues involving the booking of a hotel room are included not only in the section entitled "Making Travel Arrangements," but also in another section, "Getting Information." Similarly, in one book in the series, within the section entitled "Entertainment and Health" there is a segment in which a student describes his future work plans. This dialogue would very possibly be of interest to high school students—especially graduating seniors—yet you could easily overlook it if your method of selection depended on the table of contents, or even on skimming through the book itself.

A better means of choosing material is to use Appendix I to this Manual ("A Description of the Dialogues by Content"), which allows an at-a-glance review of the subject matter. When you find a topic of interest, you will note that it is identified by unit, page in the book, and number of the dialogue itself. If, after turning to the passage and reading it, you decide that you will play it for the class, you may wish to mark in the square next to the dialogue itself the number which appears on your tape cassette "counter." In this way you can quickly relocate the tape for future use.

An additional advantage to using the Appendix is that it can enable you to follow through, from session to session, a particular type of subject matter, or theme, which you may wish to emphasize. There would seem to be almost countless possibilities, but a few examples may suffice to illustrate that grouping tapes together according to some overriding pattern may be of interest to you.

A teacher who wanted to give the class some practice with the speech of "mass communication," for instance, would find in the contents to one edition of the series two tapes that were made from radio broadcasts (a weather forecast, as well as a commercial for car tune-ups); and beyond this other tapes presenting a more difficult level of comprehension skill (loudspeaker announcements as recorded at train stations and airports). Another teacher might wish to select according to the various types of voices recorded (e.g., the voices of children, or the voices of young people roughly the ages of those in the classroom). It might even be interesting to play several tapes involving interviews with foreigners residing in the host country of the target language, in order to get some practice in understanding foreign accents. One could also select tapes with the purpose of getting to know a particular type of person interviewed, since in some of the editions various speakers appear in numerous dialogues. It is easy to imagine that a class might want to "adopt" one particular speaker in the French edition, the charming two-year old Pierre Yves! In short, the tapes to each language program can be considered a sort of "linguistic archive," and the Appendix can serve as your guide.

Activities

Although you may prefer to just play the tapes and invite your students' reactions, a non-structured approach to the tape program can be implemented in conjunction with several fairly loosely structured activities. Here are some suggestions:

1. Discussion
After playing the tape and clarifying the difficult parts so that everyone has understood, discuss it with the class. In the beginning, use English as the language of discussion, so that the class grasps the general idea of this activity. If the activity proves successful, try to hold similar discussions in the target language. Some questions you could raise would be the following: Where did this dialogue take place, and how do we know? Are there any background sounds or clues that help us to visualize the setting? Can we determine the approximate ages of the speakers, and, if so, how? What is the mood of the speakers—relaxed or tensed? cooperative or suspicious? warm or reserved? How much information do we have about the speakers, and what questions might we have that still remain unanswered?

2. "Predictive Speech" and "Recapitulation"
Two somewhat more difficult levels of activity involve either "predictive speech" or "recapitulation." In the first (done with the book closed), play the tape, but every so often hold the "pause" button and have the class try to predict what will be said next. In the second, after first playing the tape and then having the students close their books, have the class reconstruct what was said, to the extent possible.

3. Role Playing
A more sophisticated level of activity involves the following various forms of role playing, as modeled on the tape. *a)* After playing the tape, replay it with the

books closed; then, at the points where you hold the "pause" button, volunteers, or those called upon, reenact the part of the speaker deleted and fill in the missing segments of the conversations. *b)* Reenact the tape with you, the teacher, taking the part of the interviewer, and members of the class the parts of the persons interviewed. At a later point, "step out of the picture" and have the members of the class reenact the contents of the dialogue on their own. Begin by having them remain faithful to the original version, then encourage improvisation (new answers, a new setting, a change of mood, etc.). *c)* Play the tape, and while holding the "pause" button let the bolder students play the part of on-the-spot interpreter.

Using the Tapes and Book as a Selected Grammar Review

A more structured method of integrating the *Just Listen 'n Learn* program into a previously existing curriculum is to use the material from the tapes and book as a selected grammar review, possibly (but not necessarily) in conjunction with a standard grammar textbook.

In some instances you may find that the grammar point explained may not actually recur in much depth in the dialogues to that particular unit. This is because, in contrast to a traditional textbook, in which dialogues are usually written with the express *purpose* of illustrating a specific grammatical features (e.g., the subjunctive), the same features arise in the *Just Listen 'n Learn* series only as organically related to the subject matter treated. Consequently, they may at times appear only rather sporadically.

By the same token, in certain units the subject matter itself may cause a recurrence in depth of a particular grammatical feature. To illustrate, the topics *"Tanti Anni Fa"* (Unit 13 in the Italian edition) and "Talking About the Past" (Unit 14 in the German edition and 15 in the French and Spanish editions) obviously provide concentrated practice in the various past tenses used in each language. Similarly, another section in which a grammatical point is thoroughly illustrated can be seen in "Stating Your Intentions" (Unit 14 in the French and Spanish editions, and Unit 15 in the German edition), in which the future and future perfect tenses recur repeatedly.

In summary, because of the varying nature of the subject matter in the dialogues themselves, it is advisable that after consulting Appendix II ("A Description of the Grammar Presented by Unit and a Listing of Grammatical Exercises") you also review the printed dialogues and exercises *before* playing the tapes, in order to determine how well they actually illustrate the grammatical point you wish to concentrate on.

Assuming that the dialogues you have chosen offer ample illustration of the grammatical point in question, you can profitably make use of the tapes and written exercises for two very worthwhile purposes. First, in playing the tapes, you can dramatically illustrate with "living" examples the features under study, and in so doing, provide a definitive answer to those perennial questions asked of all language teachers, such as, "But do Spaniards really *use* the subjunctive?" Secondly, in assigning the grammar exercises in *Just Listen 'n Learn* (possibly as homework) you can provide additional written practice to complement any points you may be studying in a standard grammar textbook—or, if you are no longer using one, any points which you feel need additional review.

You may wish to use the following method of presenting the material:

1. If you are using a standard grammar textbook, finish all work you are covering there first.
2. Before playing the tapes you have selected, review the printed form of the dialogue beforehand, and have the class identify the presence of the grammatical features under study, as they recur throughout the text.
3. Play and then replay the tape, using the "pause" button in order to answer questions or clarify points; then replay the tape without interruption.
4. Do in class any comprehension exercises you have selected from the unit (on the basis of Appendix III and your own study of the material), and assign any grammar exercises you think would be useful (on the basis of Appendix II, and your own review of their contents).

A Gradated Program for Developing Increasing Levels of Skill

Finally, a further structured approach to *Just Listen 'n Learn* consists of integrating the program's material into a previously established curriculum according to the various skill levels of comprehension and self-expression that you may wish to develop. The following section of this Manual consists of a list of various categories of exercises that can be employed with the tapes, arranged according to their difficulty, along with some comments on the purpose they can serve and an example from each. Most of these categories are represented in the course book (although to different degrees in the various language editions). So when you decide on a particular type of activity, you will probably find many examples to choose from in Appendix III ("A Catalogue and Description of the Comprehension Exercises According to Level of Skill Involved"), which lists all the exercises to each program, characterizes their content, and gives their location by unit, page, and exercise number. Although some of the categories to follow may not be represented in your book, you may wish to design exercises of your own.

Stay at any one level as long as you like before moving on, especially if a particular type of exercise proves successful or is enjoyed by the class. You should also feel free to skip levels or to experiment, since, as has been mentioned before, your prospects for positive results with the entire program will be greatly enhanced if you are flexible and imaginative.

1. Recording Word Frequency

The purpose of this very simple exercise is to "break the ice" when first presenting the tapes by giving students a project that they can quickly master. This in turn will help build confidence and create a receptive state of mind for future activities. The exercise can also be helpful in sensitizing students to the language as heard over the tape recorder, as well as to differences in the pronunciation, inflection, and voices of the various speakers. Procedure: Write selected words from the dialogue on the board and have students copy them on a sheet of paper. You may wish to concentrate on a particular part of speech (such as verbs, or adjectives), and you may also wish to include a few words *not* on the tape, just to make things more interesting. After the students have listened to the tape with their books open—perhaps several times—play it through again with books closed. Students are to check the word as many times as it is spoken. There are no specific exercises of this kind in your book, but if you created one based on a dialogue in Spanish, it might look something like this:

> hablo ✓
> dicen ✓✓✓
> van
> querer ✓
> saber ✓
> supo
> sabía ✓✓

2. Choral Recitation and Dictation

This exercise serves many of the same purposes of the one above, but it is more difficult, incorporating both listening and writing. Procedure: Play the tape through with books closed. Then, with or without the book (as you prefer), play a segment of the tape, hold the "pause" button, and repeat what has been said, with the class then repeating after you. At a later stage, with the books closed, begin the process again, but this time have the students repeat directly from the tape itself. Finally, playing short, manageable segments of the tape and then holding the "pause" button, have students write out the passage as a "dictation," and collect the results. Note that although there may be a few short dictations in your book, you would do best to select your own. Most dialogues will serve, but monologues, such as the following example from the French edition, would be best:

"C'est très calme. Il n'y a pas beaucoup de vie, mais la ville est très agréable parce que, en général, les gens sont gentils, sont resté simples, et les commerçants sont très agréables . . ." etc.
(from a subject interviewed on life in his native village: p. 162)

3. Rearranging the Text

This exercise involves the student's recognition of content and sequence, but does not yet require the absorbing, retention, and restating of specific information. It is often possible to do such exercises without first hearing the tape, on the basis of the written material alone. But even in such cases the tape should be played afterwards, since doing so not only confirms the correct answers but also reinforces the student's comprehension and further builds confidence. Here is a translation of an exercise contained in the Italian edition (p. 85), which is based on a specific dialogue that may be played beforehand:

"Which bus do you wish to take?"

"You're welcome."

"The stop for bus #63 is twenty meters to the right of the corner."

"Number 63."

"Good morning, Miss. Excuse me, where is the nearest bus stop?"

"Thank you very much."

4. True/False

This and subsequent exercises are now at a level of greater comprehension skills, since they require the absorption, retention, and restating of specific information.

"Ruth is asking two little boys some questions. Listen to the dialogue, then decide whether the statements below are true or false *(Richtig oder Falsch)* and tick the right box (Answers p. 34)."

a) Ruth asks the boys where they live.   R ☐   F ☐

b) The boys are called Thomas and Robert. R ☐   F ☐

c) Thomas is seven years old. (etc.)   R ☐   F ☐
(from the German edition, p. 30)

5. Multiple Choice

Similar to "True/False," yet somewhat more difficult because more than two answers can be chosen from.

"Listen as many times as you like to the conversation on tape and tick the correct answers below. (You can check your answers on p. 34.)"

a) He is
- ☐ English
- ☐ French
- ☐ American

b) He speaks French
- ☐ very well
- ☐ quite well
- ☐ very badly

c) He lives
- ☐ in England
- ☐ in France
- ☐ in America

(French edition, p. 30)

6. Checking Off Items

This exercise may be somewhat harder because it often involves two simultaneous activities, i.e., doing the exercise *while* listening to the tape.

"On the tape you will hear Jacques ordering a meal for three from the menu below in one of the *Bistros de la Gare* in Paris. Tick on the menu the items he orders."
(French edition, p. 140)

7. Fill-ins

Although in several exercises in each book only numbers need be written, generally speaking fill-ins require a somewhat higher level of skill because here the student must write in the target language.

"Gina wants to buy some things at the grocer's. Listen to her reading out her shopping list on tape and see if you can label the groceries in the picture below with their Italian name."
(Italian edition, p. 118)

Note that a slight variation of the fill-in is the **Grid,** which is identified as such in Appendix III. Students may find many of these to be particularly challenging:

"Fill in the grid below with the information on the packaging, weight *(peso)*, and cost *(prezzo)* of the various kinds of coffee mentioned in dialogue 3. Refer back to it either on p. 108 or on tape. This is not a memory exercise. Some boxes are already filled in to help you."

Marca	**Suerte**	**Splendid**	**Lavazza**	**Nescafé**	**Faemino**
Marca	Suerte	Splendid	Lavazza "oro"	Nescafé "Grand' Aroma"	Faemino "Tranquillo"
confezione	pachetto			vasetto	
peso			200 g.		
prezzo		L 1700 X			

(Italian edition, p. 113)

8. Matchings

Matchings offer a wide variety of possibilities that are more complex, and at times fairly difficult, because they involve the coordination of three elements: the aural, the visual, and the written.

"Listen to your tape, where you will hear several people being given directions. The diagrams below illustrate what each person must do. Write in the name of the person underneath the appropriate illustration. The names are: Elisa, Juana, Juan, and Pablo. (Answers on p. 76)."
(Spanish edition, p. 71)

9. Answering Informational Questions in English

In contrast to activities 4 through 9, in which the answers are supplied in one form or another (either to be chosen from written options or checked off, filled in, or matched up while listening to the tape), the following category requires retaining information that must be restated coherently. (The language of expression, however, is still English.)

"Herr Schmidt asks Frl. Johann to go to the theater with him. Listen to their conversation, then answer the questions below. (Answers p. 216)"

a) Has Herr Schmidt already bought the tickets?

b) Does Frl. Johann have time to come along?

c) What's the title of the play? (etc.)

(German edition, p. 212)

10. Supplying Missing Parts of a Conversation

We are now at the more difficult level of forming words, phrases, and complete sentences in the target language. This particular activity is still relatively elementary, however, inasmuch as the sequences required have already been formed in the dialogues and need only be repeated verbatim in exercises of this kind.

"Here's one side of a dialogue between you and a gasoline station attendant. The pictures will guide you as to what to write. (Answers on p. 132)"

"¿Sí, señora?"

"Oiga, ¿ _____ ?"

"Lo siento, sólo tenemos super o normal."

"Bueno, _____ ."

"¿Miro el aceite?"

" _____ ."

(Spanish edition, p. 128; based on a dialogue from p. 122)

11. Translating

Translating is, of course, an advanced skill, but here again the student is dealing largely with ready-made phrases from the dialogue.

"With the help of the (Italian) captions to the pictures below, complete a postcard to an old friend in Rome who couldn't join you on your holiday on the Italian Riviera, by translating the English sentences below. You don't need your tape recorder. (Answers p. 216)"

"... all the people are very nice. Every day we've been swimming and sunbathing. Sometimes we've been sailing, and on Sunday ... etc."
(Italian edition, p. 212)

12. Answering Informational Questions in the Target Language

As opposed to mere translating, this activity requires listening or reading comprehension, and a broader use of the target language.

"Imagine you are the woman whose morning routine is illustrated below. Answer the questions you will hear on the tape about what you will be doing tomorrow. Say your answer out loud and also write it in the gap provided. (Answers p. 200)"
(French edition, p. 195)

13. Reenacting a Dialogue

Although somewhat similar to the above type of exercise, reenacting a dialogue may often prove more difficult because the "answers" will not necessarily be those originally heard on the tape. The student may be required to provide answers based on playing the role of himself or herself, but sometimes a new and unfamiliar role may be assigned, as in the example below:

> "A customs officer *(un aduanero)* is interviewing two people at the airport in Madrid. From the information supplied, work out how they would answer the following questions. First, fill in their replies, then listen to the cassette, where you will hear the full dialogue."
>
> José García: a Spaniard, a teacher of French and English, from Madrid.
>
> Ruth Saddler: José's fiancée, English, hairdresser from London, works in Madrid.
>
> Aduanero: "¿Nombre, por favor?"
>
> José: "_____."
>
> Aduanero: "¿ _____?"
>
> José: "_____."

(Spanish edition, p. 15)

14. Class Discussion

At the most potentially sophisticated level of activity, any number of dialogues can lend themselves to class discussion, as has already been mentioned earlier (see the "Activities" section under "A Non-structured Approach). You may wish to do a trial run for this type of activity in English first, and later discuss a subsequent dialogue in the target language itself. None of the books contains discussion exercises per se, but all have many dialogues that would provide good material. In looking through Appendix I ("A Description of the Dialogues by Content"), you will find these subjects, which will provide one example for each edition of the series:

French: In Unit 12, dialogues 1 through 6, various speakers compare the country life of their native villages to city life in Paris. Discussion topic: What are the advantages and disadvantages of country and city living in both France and the United States?

German: In Unit 13, dialogue 2, a man and a woman describe their many hobbies. Discussion topic: Which members of the class share the same hobbies and why?

Italian: In Unit 15, dialogue 2, a woman applies for a refund on an unused train ticket, but the employee explains why she cannot have her money back. Discussion topic: Was the woman treated fairly?

Spanish: In Unit 11, dialogue 6, a husband tells why he refuses to do housework, which he calls "women's work." (In all fairness, it should be pointed out that his attitudes are probably far less typical today than among his fellow countrymen in past eras.) In any case, a discussion of whether his point of view is justified would certainly prove lively in an American classroom!

15. Miscellaneous

A final category of activity which can only be termed "miscellaneous" has also been included in Appendix III. This category, which represents a wide range of skill levels, contains many challenging exercises that your class may enjoy. To cite some examples, the student is variously required to solve a crossword puzzle; to fill in forms such as a hotel registration and the application for opening a bank account; and to follow taped instructions with reference to a map in the book in order to see where he or she ends up.

Appendix I: A Description of the Dialogues by Content

Notes:
The following provides an at-a-glance inventory of the content of all the taped dialogues in your book. They are listed below their unit heading, and identified by their numbers. When the subject matter to various dialogues in a unit is similar, they have been grouped together.

French

Unit 1: Talking about yourself

1-3 speakers exchange greetings at different times of day

4 segments illustrating "please"

5 a mother tries to get her child to count

6, 7 people identify their nationalities and cities

Unit 2: Yourself and others

1 people asked if they work, and where

2 six speakers state their occupations

3 a couple about to celebrate a wedding anniversary

4 a man describes the members of his family and tells the names of his children

5 a woman tells of her family, her work as a secretary, and her boss

6 a woman refuses a date

7 counting from 1 to 20

Unit 3: Ordering drinks and snacks

1 a hotel employee takes a breakfast order by phone

2 a waiter describes choices for breakfast

3 choices of liquor and soft drinks at a hotel bar

4 ordering an apéritif

5-7 ordering snacks at a café

8 ordering pancakes

9 a child tells why he likes tea

Unit 4: Getting information

1, 2 a hotel receptionist take reservations by phone

3 booking a hotel room

4 booking a campsite

5 asking the location of the washroom

6 cashing traveler's checks

7 a child gives the French version of the sounds made by animals

8 the same child describes his ideal lunch

Unit 5: Directions

1, 2 how to get to the train station

3, 4 directions to Bayeux; directions at a campsite

5, 6 taking the subway to the Eiffel Tower and to Notre Dame

7 why a passenger takes a particular type of train

8 the location of a bank

9 finding things in one's hotel

Unit 6: Time

1 an employee at the airport

2 the last bus to the concert

3 an employee gives train schedules

4 schedules at a camping ground

5 a schoolgirl's typical day

6, 7 girls describe school holidays and summer vacation

Unit 7: Shopping (Part I)

Purchases of newspapers (1); stamps (2); bread (3); a bottle of wine (4); groceries (5); fruit and vegetables (6); making an appointment at the beauty parlor (7)

Unit 8: Shopping (Part II)

Shopping at a pharmacy (1); buying socks for a child (2); buying a sweater (3); flowers (4); fruit juice (5)

Unit 9: Making travel arrangements

1 booking a flight
2 ways to get to Bayeux
3-6 buying train tickets to Soulac, Nice, and Nantes
7 a check-up at a gas station

Unit 10: Food and drink

1 a long dialogue on ordering a meal
2 deciding whether to order à la carte
3 deciding what to eat at a café
4 people describe what they had for lunch

Unit 11: Likes and dislikes

1-7 seven speakers describe their tastes in food
8-10 speakers describe their native villages and comment on Paris
11 a man describes a family he lived with in London

Unit 12: Your town—the weather

1-6 speakers compare life in five French cities
7 a speaker describes the differences in weather throughout France

Unit 13: More about yourself

1-4 speakers describe their houses and apartments
5 a child receives a present
6 a man's trip to Africa
7 a woman tells how she learned two foreign languages

Unit 14: Stating your intentions

1 a young woman plans to be a journalist
2 a man tells what he will do tomorrow
3 the same man describes his new job
4 the tasks a woman must complete when she returns to Paris
5 a child tells how old he is

Unit 15: Talking about the past

1 a trip to England

2 a woman tells what she did yesterday

3, 4 a yacht trip from France to Morocco

5 a vacation on the Côte d'Azur

German

Unit 1: Talking about yourself

1 two people introduced to one another

2 a man introduces his family

3, 4 introductions exchanged with two more couples

5 a train passenger is interviewed

6, 7 various foreigners residing in Germany introduce themselves

8 an employee asks interviewer her name and address

9 a little girl recites the alphabet

Unit 2: Yourself and others

1-3 a man and two women describe their families

4, 5 two men state their occupations and knowledge of languages

6a a loudspeaker is tested by means of counting

6b a child recites a German counting rhyme

7, 8 people tell how long they've been at present locations

Unit 3: Getting information

1-3 booking a hotel room

4, 5 as above, at a different hotel

6 the locations of the nearest bank

7, 8 changing money at the bank

Unit 4: Ordering drinks and snacks

1 ordering breakfast

2 at the bakery

3-7 ordering drinks and snacks at a café

Unit 5: Directions
1-3 asking directions at a streetcar stop
4 stops called from the streetcar
5-7 questions at the tourist office
8, 9 getting directions from passersby

Unit 6: Time
1 what time is it?
2 a radio station announces the time
3, 4 asking the schedules of a museum and a bar
5 a woman tells when she takes vacations, and where
6 a song about the seasons

Unit 7: Shopping (Part I)
Shopping for postcards (1); souvenirs (2); bread (3); fruits and vegetables (4); and jewelry (5, 6)

Unit 8: Shopping (Part II)
1 at the supermarket the check-out clerk calls off items and prices
2, 3 shopping for shoes
4, 5 at the pharmacy

Unit 9: Making travel arrangements
1, 2 loudspeaker announcements at the train station
3, 4 buying train tickets
5-7 at the train station information desk

Unit 10: Ordering a meal
1-3 finding good, inexpensive restaurants
4 asking about the local cuisine
5, 6 ordering food and wine in a restaurant

Unit 11: Likes and dislikes

1, 2 local residents, including foreigners, give impressions of Ulm

3 a man compares northern and southern Germany

4 people state preferences in food and travel

5 where Germans like to vacation, both at home and abroad

Unit 12: Your town—the weather

1 at the tourist office: sights to see in Freiburg

2, 3 a woman describes her native city and what people do for recreation there

4 a man describes his city, which we must guess

5 a weather report on the radio

Unit 13: More about yourself

1 two young boys fishing on the Danube describe their "catch"!

2 a man and woman describe their many hobbies

3 where a man lived before, and where he lives now

4 a schoolteacher talks at some length about why his new apartment is better than where he lived before (monologue)

Unit 14: Talking about the past

1 a young woman describes a vacation in India, and what it's like to travel alone

2, 3 how a German man took a group of English students to Berlin and the nightlife they enjoyed

4 a narrator tells about an interesting 19th century local figure from Ulm, a tailor who tried to fly

Unit 15: Stating your intentions

1 how a working woman will spend her day off

2 a man invites a woman to a concert

3 plans for the weekend

4 two women describe their vacation plans

5 an upcoming vacation in Latin America

6 a women describes plans for her career and raising children

Italian

Unit 1: Talking about yourself
1 greetings exchanged on the telephone
2 a social introduction
3-5 clearing customs
6 five Italian students introduce themselves

Unit 2: Travel information
1, 2 loudspeaker announcements at the train station
3 interviews of travelers on a train
4 loudspeaker announcements at the airport
5 checking baggage at the airport
6 a tourist office employee gives out phone numbers

Unit 3: Accommodation—more about yourself
1, 2 interviews of travelers on a train
3 booking a hotel room
4 a customer shops for a jumper
5-7 asking location of department stores and a public telephone

Unit 4: Ordering drinks and snacks
1 hotel accommodations and room prices
2 are traveler's checks and credit cards accepted?
3 information at the hotel registration desk
4 a waiter describes choices for breakfast
5 ordering drinks at the hotel bar
6 a snack vendor on the train describes what he sells

Unit 5: Directions
1-8 asking directions to a department store; the nearest bank; a foreign currency exchange; a *piazza*
9 taking public transportation to a park
10 a woman who can't give directions

Unit 6: Time

1 asking about a train schedule at the information office

2, 3 loudspeaker announcements at the train station and the airport

4 the hotel receptionist tells when breakfast is served

5 getting directions to a tourist attraction in another city

6, 7 opening and closing times for a bank and for local shops

Unit 7: Shopping (Part I)

Questions and purchases at a bakery (1, 2); a newsstand (3); at the post office (4); a perfume counter (5); a tobacco shop (6)

Unit 8: Shopping (Part II)

Questions and purchases at a bakery (1); a grocery store (2); a boutique (4, 5); a perfume counter (6)

Unit 9: Making travel arrangements

1, 2, 6 buying train tickets

3, 4 getting information at the ticket window

5 an employee describes the various types of trains used in the Italian railway system

Unit 10: Food and drink

1-3 talking with a waiter

5, 6 a waiter describes items on the menu

4 ordering how you wish your meat cooked

7 a description of the wine list

Unit 11: Likes and dislikes

1 a waiter describes appetizers

2 ordering a dinner

3 two friends discuss their favorite flowers

4 a hotel receptionist offers a choice of rooms

5 Italian students who have lived in England compare their impressions of English and Italian food

Unit 12: Car travel—the weather

1, 2 a radio advertisement for car tune-ups

3 a gas station attendant describes his interactions with non-Italian-speaking tourists

4 a chat about the weather

5 a radio weather forecast

Unit 13: More about yourself

1-3 interviews with Italians about their experiences in English-speaking countries

4 a waiter describes his work

5 two Italians describe their home towns

Unit 14: Entertainment—health

1 a young couple makes plans for the evening

2 two friends plan to go to the opera

3 a youth describes his future work plans

4 a speaker describes an upcoming vacation

5 a pharmacist offers recommendations for curing a headache

6 a father takes his child to the doctor

Unit 15: Solving problems

1 cashing a check at a bank

2 a woman is refused a refund on her unused train ticket

3 a writer recalls her past

4 a speaker describes his last vacation and some problems he had with the hotel bill

Spanish

Unit 1: Talking about yourself

1-4 children and adults are asked where they are from

6-8 various adults tell something about themselves

9 a woman introduces people to one another

10 a child is asked what language he speaks

Unit 2: Yourself and others

1-3, 5 interviews with several children

4 a woman talks about her children

6 asking directions in a department store

7 a foreign woman has some difficulty understanding

Unit 3: Getting information

1 a Spaniard describes his home

2, 3 asking the location of a pharmacy and the washroom

4 a speaker describes objects on a table

5, 6 booking a hotel room; booking a campsite

7 two women compare apartment living to hotel living

Unit 4: Ordering drinks and snacks

1 a child is asked to count her money aloud

2 a waiter is asked for the check

3 a speaker counts coins on a table

4, 5 a meal with a Spanish family

6 ordering drinks and snacks at a café

Unit 5: Directions

1 asking people the meaning of various road signs

2 asking the distances to various cities

3-6 asking directions to various streets and plazas

7 asking a service station attendant how to get to Madrid

Unit 6: Time

1 asking the time of day

2 a speaker describes the hours a building remains open

3-6 inquiring as to departures, arrivals, and travel times of trains and buses

7 placing an overseas phone call

8 a woman is asked the identity of famous people in photographs

9 a woman states her birthday and saint's day

Unit 7: Shopping (Part I)

Purchases of batteries for a tape recorder (1); milk and olive oil (2); items at a grocery store (3); souvenirs (4); a suitcase (5)

Unit 8: Shopping (Part II)

Purchases of sports equipment (1); a *mantilla* and a headscarf (2, 3); a man's jacket and slacks (4, 5); paying with a credit card (6); purchasing a dress (7); asking about medicine at a pharmacy (8)

Unit 9: Making travel arrangements

1 a child describes how to get to his school

2, 3 hailing taxis

4, 5 stopping at a gas station; getting a flat tire fixed

6 buying a train ticket

Unit 10: Food and drink

1, 2 asking about local restaurants and their ratings

3-5 ordering a meal and dessert

6 ordering drinks

Unit 11: Likes and dislikes

1 a woman describes what sort of housework she likes and dislikes

2 the same woman's preferences in food and drink

3, 4 her feelings about Spain and its various regions

5 a Spanish woman gives her impressions of England

6 a Spanish man who refuses to do housework

Unit 12: The weather

1-4 several Spaniards discuss the climate of their native regions

5 a tourist describes his preference for the weather of Spain

6, 7 an explanation of seasonal tourist rates and various types of accommodations

Unit 13: More about yourself

Descriptions of a typical work day by a young man and woman (1, 2); the school day of a small boy (3); the activities of a retired man (4); a typical day of the interviewer (5); planning a family outing (6)

Unit 14: Stating your intentions

1 two speakers make plans for the evening

2 a woman describes how she will spend her Saturday

3 a man describes an errand he must carry out

4 a hairdresser describes how he will cut a woman's hair

5, 6 asking directions to the beach, and to a village

7 a man describes his plans for tomorrow

Unit 15: Talking about the past

1 a Spanish woman describes a trip to England

2 a housewife recalls the activities of her day

3 a man tells how his car broke down

4 a man tells of his outing to the beach

5, 6 a woman tells of her vacation last year

7 inquiring about flight arrivals at the airport

Japanese _____

Unit 1: Talking about yourself

1 speakers greet each other and introduce themselves

2 speakers greet and take leave of each other

3 speakers exchange small talk

4 a speaker introduces one friend to another

Unit 2: Yourself and others

1 an adult asks a child to count and give some dates and month names

2 an adult asks a child for days of the week

3 two speakers talk about their places of origin

4　a speaker asks a new friend personal questions

5　two women talk about their families

6　two speakers talk about their work

Unit 3: Ordering drinks and snacks

1　a customer orders a snack at a restaurant

2　a married couple discuss what to eat for lunch

3　a man places a restaurant order for himself and his wife

4　a restaurant customer settles the bill with the cashier

Unit 4: Getting information

1　a speaker vainly tries to make a hotel reservation

2　a speaker checks into a hotel

3　the desk clerk asks the guest's checkout time

4　a hotel guest is directed to his room

Unit 5: Directions

1　a student asks the way in a train station

2　a clerk gives detailed directions on how to find a post office

3　a tourist asks a clerk directions to Meiji Shrine

4　a customer conducts business at a cleaners

Unit 6: Time

1　a speaker asks about the business hours of a department store

2　two speakers agree to meet for a date

3　two speakers agree on a time to go shopping

4　a speaker asks another how long he has been in Tokyo

Unit 7: Shopping (Part I)

1　a clerk totals a purchase

2　a customer asks a clerk to reserve a golf trophy

3　a customer asks a pharmacist to recommend medicines for a trip

4　a customer conducts various transactions at a post office

Unit 8: Shopping (Part II)

1 a customer checks the availability of various colors for a blouse and asks to have it gift-wrapped

2 a customer asks a pharmacist about medicine for a sore throat

3 a customer arranges shipping and payment by credit card

4 a woman plans her grocery shopping for a picnic

Unit 9: Making travel arrangements

1 a woman reports on her trip to Kyoto

2 a woman explains the best way to get to Akihabara

3 a traveler discusses ticketing options for a trip to Kyoto

4 a customer discusses prices for hot-springs accommodations

Unit 10: Food and drink

1 a host offers tea to a friend

2 a hotel guest explores options and places an order with room service

3 two people discuss getting something to eat

4 two people discuss the kind of restaurant they would like to go to

Unit 11: Likes and dislikes

1 a speaker describes a trip to Eastern Europe

2 a speaker discusses an upcoming trip to Kyoto

3 a tourist describes his hotel and some of his sightseeing

4 a woman discusses her painting hobby

Unit 12: The weather

1 two people discuss the terrible weather during rainy season

2 two people say goodbye; they discuss what the weather will be like when they meet again

3 an announcer gives the weather forecast

4 a travel agent talks about the best time to visit Japan

Unit 13: My daily routine

1 a speaker describes a day's activities

2 two speakers discuss sports activities

3 two people discuss housing in Tokyo
4 an apartment seeker makes inquiries at a real estate agency

Unit 14: Stating your intentions

1 one person asks to join another for a trip to the art museum
2 two tourists make plans for their day
3 two people discuss going to see Kabuki
4 a customer discusses a trip to Europe at a travel agency

Unit 15: Talking about the past

1 two people discuss the languages they have studied
2 a husband tells his wife about his day
3 a speaker expresses surprise that a foreign visitor found a hotel room too small
4 a speaker describes his foreign friend's experience at a noodle shop

Russian

Unit 1: Talking about yourself

1–2 speakers exchange greetings
3–4 speakers introduce themselves to each other
5 a student introduces a friend to his mother
6 a student asks another his surname
7 speakers take leave of each other

Unit 2: Talking about yourself and others

1–2 speakers ask about each other's families
3–5 speakers talk about their professions
6 a student asks another where he lives
7 a speaker gives his work and home phone numbers
9 a speaker asks a stranger for directions to a subway station

Unit 3: Asking for and receiving information

1–2 a woman checks into a hotel
3 a man checks into a hotel without a reservation
4 a woman changes some money

Unit 4: Ordering drinks and snacks

1–2 a woman selects breakfast at a friend's house

3–6 two women order lunch at the office cafeteria

7 a man asks a stranger where a fast lunch is served

Unit 5: Getting what you want in shops (Part I)

1–2 a woman buys stamps and postcards

3 a woman buys a newspaper at a hotel kiosk

4 a woman gets tickets to the Bolshoi Theater

5–7 a woman buys some groceries

8 a woman selects among tomatoes of different prices

Unit 6: Getting what you want in shops (Part II)

1–2 a woman asks about items and their prices at a shop

3 a woman buys some flowers from a street vendor

4–5 a woman finds her place in line

6 a man buys some fruit juice

7 a man buys some medicines

Unit 7: Understanding and asking about time

1–4 various speakers ask the time of day

5 a woman asks about a shop's hours

6 a woman asks about a delayed train

7 a student describes his weekly school routine

8 the same student describes some vacation activities

Unit 8: Asking for and understanding directions

1 a woman asks directions to a post office

2 a man asks directions to a street and a museum

3 a woman asks what trolleys to take to a museum

4 a woman asks what transportation to use to get to a square

5–6 a man asks how to get to a cemetery

7 a man excuses his way to a streetcar exit

Unit 9: Making travel arrangements

1–2 a woman makes rail-travel arrangements to Zagorsk
3 a woman asks a stranger about a train schedule
4–5 a woman checks Aeroflot flights to St. Petersburg
6–7 a woman inquires about renting a car

Unit 10: Ordering a meal

1–2 a woman orders a meal at a cooperative café
3–4 a man makes reservations at a café
5–7 the same man places his orders and pays the bill

Unit 11: Expressing likes and dislikes

1–2 a woman asks two students about their studies and activities
3 a girl talks about her favorite time of year
4 a fussy girl declines unsatisfactory varieties of coffee and tea
5 a woman is asked about where she lives
6 a man is asked his opinion of Moscow
7 a man is asked why he likes a certain medieval town

Unit 12: Talking about your town and the weather

1 a man talks about his native Moscow
2 the same man talks about what he likes to do in Moscow
3 a woman makes a formal announcement of a bus tour
4–5 a man talks about Moscow weather
6 a woman talks about her usual vacations

Unit 13: Giving more information about yourself

1–2 two people talk about their sport activities
3 a woman talks about her favorite pastimes
4 a woman talks about her busy life
5 a man describes the layout and contents of his home

Unit 14: Stating your intentions

1 a woman talks about her vacation plans
2 a man talks about his plans to visit Denmark

3 a man talks about his plan to buy an apartment

4 a student talks about his career ambitions

5 a student talks about her work and studies

6 a man invites a woman to go to the theater

Unit 15: Discussing what you have done

1 a woman talks about her day's touring

2 a teacher talks about an early twentieth-century satirist

3 an editor talks about his newspaper

4 a woman talks about her vacation last year

5 a woman asks a man about his trip to Germany

Greek

Unit 1: Talking about yourself

1–4 speakers exchange greetings and introduce themselves

5 a tourist presents herself at Greek customs

6 two tourists meet on the beach

7–8 speakers introduce themselves

Unit 2: Yourself and others

1 a woman asks a child personal questions

2 a man and woman exchange pleasantries

3 a woman asks another what her job is

4 a woman and man talk about their jobs

5 a woman introduces her sister to another woman

6 a woman introduces a friend to her mother

7 a man asks a woman personal questions

8 a child counts to twenty

Unit 3: Ordering drinks and snacks

1 a woman asks permission to sit next to another

2 a woman orders coffee

3 a woman orders Greek coffee and cheese pies

4 a woman asks about *ouzo* and its price

5 two women order breakfast
6 a man makes purchases at a bakery
7 two women decide to get a snack
8 two children buy ice cream at the beach
9 a speaker counts from 21 to 30 and by tens to 50

Unit 4: Getting information

1 a woman asks directions to a discotheque
2 a woman asks the way to a bar
3 a boy counts by tens to 100 and directs a man to the hotel office
4 a woman changes some dollars to drachmas
5 a woman cashes some travelers' checks
6 a woman asks another to speak more slowly
7 a woman checks into a hotel
8 a woman checks into a hotel with her children

Unit 5: Directions

1 a child asks a woman for directions to the post office
2 a woman in a bar asks where the toilet is
3 a woman asks directions to a bank
4–5 a woman asks directions to a pharmacy and the tourist office
6 a woman asks directions to the bus stop
7 a woman asks a fellow passenger what bus stop to use
8 a man asks where the OTE is
9 a woman asks the way back to her hotel
10–11 a woman asks a man directions to the post office and a street
12 a child counts by tens from 110 to 500; two women arrange to go out

Unit 6: Time

1 a woman asks another the time
2 a woman asks about the departure of her flight
3 a woman asks when her hotel serves meals
4 two children recite the days of the week and months of the year
5 a woman asks another for the date and the day of the week
6 a woman asks about boat departure times

7 a woman asks when she should be at the airport for her flight

8 a woman asks another about business hours at the shops

9 a man invites a woman for a ride in his car

10 a woman asks another the day and date

Unit 7: Shopping (Part I)

1 a boy buys bread at a bakery

2 a woman buys matches

3 a man buys stamps at a newsstand

4 a woman makes various purchases at a newsstand

5 a woman buys stamps

6 a woman buys cigarettes and matches

7 a woman buys a yellow toy car at a newsstand

8 a child buys rackets for the beach

Unit 8: Shopping (Part II)

1 a woman buys aspirin at a pharmacy

2 a man buys toothpaste at a pharmacy

3 a woman tries to find matching buttons

4 a man buys olives at the open market

5 a grocer tabulates a customer's purchases

6 a woman arranges to have her groceries delivered

7 a man buys an embroidered dress

8 a woman buys an embroidered blouse

Unit 9: Making travel arrangements

1 a woman gives a taxi driver directions

2 a man arranges to rent a car

3 a man buys a train ticket to Larisa

4 a man asks if the boat has a restaurant

5 a woman arranges an excursion at the tourist agency

6 a woman buys gasoline and has a tire changed

7 a garage attendant checks the oil and fills the tank

8 a woman asks how far it is from Athens to Kifissia

Unit 10: Food and drink

1. a woman asks to be recommended to a good bar
2. a woman orders a *mousaká* and wine
3. a woman discusses what food to order with her son
4. a woman orders several dishes
5. a woman orders hors d'œuvres
6. a waitress suggests salad and recommends the fish highly

Unit 11: Likes and dislikes

1. a man asks a woman about her food and sports preferences
2. two women discuss their favorite foods
3. a man and a woman discuss the weather in the rain
4. two people talk about Greek foods
5. a man and a woman discuss going to Nafplio in the hot weather

Unit 12: More about yourself

1. a woman asks another about her and her husband's language ability
2. a man asks a woman how she likes Athens
3. a child asks a woman some personal questions
4. a woman asks another some personal questions
5. a man and a woman get acquainted
6. a man asks a woman some personal questions
7. a woman expresses admiration of another's baby

Unit 13: The Greek alphabet

1. a woman asks directions to the nearest telephone
2. a woman asks for a telephone and a telephone directory
3. a girl asks to use the newsstand's telephone
4. a boy is shown a newsstand where he can make a phone call
5. a man makes a quick phone call from the airport
6. a woman makes travel arrangements by phone
7. a child recites the alphabet

Unit 14: Talking about the past

1 two women talk about what they did yesterday

2 a woman tells what she did at a party

3 a man asks a woman about her London visit

4 a man and a woman compare their activities of last night

5 a man and a woman compare shopping trips

6 a woman complains to another about not coming when she expected her

Unit 15: Stating your intentions

1 a woman and a man share their plans for tomorrow

2 a woman tells another of a planned trip to England

3 a man asks a woman what they will do tomorrow

4 a woman asks a man what they will do tomorrow

5 two people discuss their upcoming vacation

6 a man reads a woman's horoscope

Arabic

Unit 1: Talking about yourself

1–2 speakers exchange greetings

3 a man tells his name

4 a man answers questions about his children

5 a man applies for a job

Unit 2: Yourself and others

1 two people meet in a city café

2 two men exchange names

3 a man answers questions about his impressions of Jordan

4 a man tells where he is from

Unit 3: Ordering drinks and snacks

1 several people accept offers of tea

2 a man orders breakfast at a restaurant

3 a man clarifies a restaurant bill

4–5 a man orders a morning snack at a restaurant

Unit 4: Getting information (Part I)

1–3 a man makes a hotel reservation

4–5 a man presents himself at an office without an appointment

Unit 5: Directions

1–2 a woman asks an older man for directions

3–4 a man asks for directions

Unit 6: Time

1 several people find out the time of day

2–3 a man finds out an office's weekly hours

4 a man asks another how long he has been at his job

Unit 7: Shopping (Part I)

Purchases of a tourist guide and stamps (1); film (2–3); groceries (4)

Unit 8: Shopping (Part II)

Purchases of gifts (1); cushions (2); jewelry (3–4)

Unit 9: Making travel arrangements

1 a man investigates taxi fares

2 a man finds out where the British Council is

3–4 a student asks about and negotiates a long taxi ride

5 the same student arranges a two-stage trip from Al-Azraq to Irbid

Unit 10: Ordering a meal

1–4 two men ask detailed questions about a menu and place their order

Unit 11: Likes and dislikes

1 two men agree that they dislike leisurely mornings

2 the same men discuss the problem of finding a taxi

3 the same men share a liking for sports

4 a woman tells a friend about a reunion she enjoyed

5 a woman expresses annoyance at people trampling plants at a park

Unit 12: Arranging a meeting

1 a student makes an appointment with the British Council representative

2–3 two secretaries arrange for their employers to meet

Unit 13: Getting information (Part II)

1 a woman asks about round-trip fares to Ma'im

2 a woman asks about the exhibits and regulations of a museum

3 a student gets details about joining a library

Unit 14: Invitations and intentions

1 a man declines another man's invitation to a film

2 two men agree to have dinner together

3 a man gives reasons for declining an invitation to dinner

4 two women discuss family vacation plans

Unit 15: Talking about the past

1 a woman tells another about her weekend

2 a woman tells a man about her enjoyable weekend at a spa

3 a man describes learning to like English food

Appendix II: A Description of the Grammar Presented by Unit and Listing of Grammatical Exercises

Notes:
The purpose of this Appendix, which amplifies the section entitled *Grammar in the Course* at the back of your book, is to provide a brief yet thorough summary of the grammar points that are explained in each unit. Examples are provided when relevant, and any exercises on the grammatical material referred to are indicated by page number. If the same or a similar grammar point or exercise occurs in another unit as well, or in the *Revision/Review* section, it is cross-referenced. If a grammatical explanation in a unit is complemented by the *Grammar Summary* in the back of the book, that too is cross-referenced.

French

Unit 1

Gender of nouns
Indefinite article
Adjective agreement with nouns (see p. 101)
Present tense of *être*
Notes on subject pronouns

Unit 2

Present tense of verbs ending in *-er;* the verb *avoir,* Ex. p. 32
The partitive *(des)*
Forming negatives *(ne . . . pas),* Ex. p. 31

Unit 3

Definite article
Article combined with prepositions *(du, des),* Ex. p. 45
Present tense of *prendre, comprendre, apprendre*
Idiom: "qu'est-ce que . . . ?"

Unit 4

Forming questions ("est-ce que/qu'... ?"; "où est... ?"; "où sont... ?") Ex. p. 59
  (See also Unit 12)
Present tense of *faire, vendre*

Unit 5

Present tense of *aller*
Idiom: "il faut"
Prepositions *(sur, sous, à, de,* etc.*)* and how combined with the definite article *(près de + le = près du,* etc.*)* Two exercises, p. 73

Unit 6

Present tense of *venir* and related verbs, Ex. p. 87
Contractions *(au, aux)*

Unit 7

Expression: "je voudrais"
Present tense of *pouvoir, savoir, connaître*
Position and agreement of adjectives (see also p. 17)

Unit 8

Demonstratives *(ce, cet, cette, ces)*, Ex. p. 115
Adjectives in degrees *(grand, plus grand; bon, meilleur,* etc.*)*

Unit 9

Possessive adjectives *(notre, nos; votre, vos)*, Ex. p. 129 (See also Unit 11, Unit 14, and *Grammar Summary,* P. 224)
Two verbs together ("J'espère venir," etc.)
Present tense of *dire, partir*

Unit 10

The particle *en* (e.g., "prenez-en!"), Ex. p. 143
Present tense of *voir, finir*

Unit 11

Possessive adjectives *(mon, ma, mes; ton, ta, tes)*, Ex. p. 157 (See also Unit 9, Unit 14 and *Grammar Summary,* p. 224)
The use of *personne*
Imperfect tense of verb *être*, Ex. p. 157

Unit 12

Expressions for weather, Ex. p. 169
Interrogatives *(où? quand? comment?* etc.*)*
Inverted verbs ("quand partez-vous?" etc.)
  (See also Unit 4)

Unit 13

The present perfect tense; the auxiliary verb *avoir*, Ex. p. 183
  (See also Revision Ex., p. 218)

Unit 14

Possessive adjectives *(son, sa, ses)*, Ex. p. 197
  (See also Unit 9, Unit 11, and *Grammar Summary*, p. 224)

Unit 15

Present perfect tense with auxiliary verb *être*, Ex. p. 209
  (See also *Revision* Ex., p. 218)

German

Unit 1

Subject pronouns; familiar and polite forms for "you"
  (See also *Grammar Summary*, p. 224)
Present tense of *sein*, Ex. p. 17

Unit 2

Present tense of *haben*, Ex. p. 31
Present tense of regular verbs
Occupations in masculine and feminine forms *(ein Schüler, eine Schülerin)*

Unit 3

The concept of gender in nouns
The concept of cases
Definite and indefinite article (nominative and accusative cases)
  (See also *Grammar Summary*, p. 224)

Unit 4

Guidelines for the pluralization of nouns, Ex. p. 59

Unit 5

Guidelines for prepositions and the cases which govern them
 (See also *Grammar Summary*, p. 225)

Unit 6

Negations (use of *nicht*), Ex. p. 87

Unit 7

Guidelines for adjective endings; a list of useful adjectives

Unit 8

Adjectives in degrees', regular *(klein, kleiner, am kleinsten)* and irregular *(gut, besser, am besten)*; a list of examples.
(See also Unit 12)

Unit 9

Modal verbs *(müssen, wollen, können, möchten)*; their conjugations and some
 examples of usage

Unit 10

Expression: "es gibt"; idiomatic uses, Ex. p. 143

Unit 11

Expressions for "to like" *(gefallen; gern, lieber, am liebsten)*

Unit 12

Comparisons of equality *(als)* and of degree *(klein, kleiner, am kleinsten)*,
 Ex. p. 171
(See also Unit 8)

Unit 13

The perfect tense ("ich habe gewohnt," etc.), Ex. p. 185

Unit 14

The imperfect tense; weak verbs ("ich wohnte") and strong verbs ("ich kam"); conjugations of *sein* and *haben* in perfect and imperfect tenses.

Unit 15

The future tense

Italian

Unit 1

Concept of gender and number
Forms of the demonstrative *(questo, questa, questi, queste)* Ex. p. 16
Plural of nouns ending in *o* and *a*
Present tense of verbs ending in *-are*, Ex. p. 17
Present tense of *avere, essere*

Unit 2

Definite article; forms in the singular, Ex. p. 30
Article combined with prepositions; forms in the singular *(del*, etc.*)*
Present tense of *venire, andare*, Ex. p. 31

Unit 3

Plural of nouns ending in *e*
Indefinite article
Present tense of *fare, sapere*
Reflexive verbs *(chiamarsi, trattenersi*, etc.*)*

Unit 4

Definite article; forms in the plural, Ex. p. 59
Article combined with prepositions; forms in the plural *(dei*, etc.*)*, Ex. p. 43
Present tense of *potere volere*
Object pronouns
 (See also *Grammar Summary*, p. 228)

Unit 5

Present tense of *dovere, uscire*
Spelling changes with plural forms *(il banco, i banchi*, etc.*)*
Irregular plurals *(amico, amici,* etc.*)*, Ex. p. 73

Unit 6

Present tense of verbs ending in *-ire*
Interrogatives *(quanto? quale? quando?)*, Ex. p. 87
Expressions of time *(oggi, domani, dopodomani,* etc.*)*, Ex. p. 87

Unit 7

Direct object pronouns: third person forms *(lo, la, li, le)*, Ex. p. 101
  (See also *Grammar Summary*, p. 228)
Comparisons *(più, meno, così... come,* etc.*)*, Ex. p.101

Unit 8

Formation of the past participle; its use as an adjective
Present tense of verbs ending in *-ire* with infix *sc (finire, capire)*
Special uses of *piacere* for "to like"
  (See also Unit 11, p. 156, and *Revision* Ex. p. 221)

Unit 9

Third person phrases *(basta, bisogna, ci vuole* etc.*)*, Ex. p. 127
Formation of adverbs, Ex. p. 128

Unit 10

The superlative *-issimo,* Ex. p. 143
Recognizing shortened words *(l'auto* for *l'automomobile,* etc.*)*

Unit 11

Present tense of *scegliere*
Possessive adjectives *(il mio, il tuo, il suo,* etc.*)*, Ex. p. 156
  (See also *Revision* Ex. p. 222)

Unit 12

Future tense, *Revision* Ex. p. 223
Present perfect tense

Unit 13

Imperfect tense, Exercises pp. 183-4 (on all tenses introduced
  in Units 12 and 13)

Unit 14
Conditional tense, Ex. p. 199

Unit 15
Further uses of the imperfect
Use of *venire* and *andare* as auxiliary verbs
Special uses of preposition *da*

Spanish

Unit 1
Present tense of *ser;* its use
Present tense of verbs ending in *-ar (hablar, estudiar)*
Gender of nouns
Definite article: singular forms

Unit 2
Present tense of *vender, tener*
Pluralization of nouns
Present tense of *estar;* its use

Unit 3
Present tense of *vivir, preferir*
Expression: *hay*
Indefinite article; its plural forms with meaning of "some" *(unos, unas)*

Unit 4
Forming questions by changing voice inflection
Forming questions by word inversion
Interrogatives *(¿cuánto? ¿cómo?* etc.) and their use
Porque as "because" and *¿por qué?* as "why?"
Present tense of *querer*
Numbers: counting through 100 and beyond
  (See also *Grammar Summary*, pp. 224–225

Unit 5
Expression: *¿se puede?*
Por vs. *para*, Ex. p. 73

Unit 6

Demonstratives *(este, ese; aquel,* etc.*)*
Telling time by the 24-hour clock
Days of the week; months of the year; stating the date

Unit 7

Adjectives and adverbs in degrees: regular forms *(caro, más caro, el más caro)* and irregular forms *(bueno, mejor)*
Present tense of *hacer*

Unit 8

Present tense and uses of *poder, saber, conocer*
Direct object pronouns: third person forms *(lo, la, los, las)*
  (See also *Grammar Summary*, p. 222)

Unit 9

Present tense of verbs ending in *-ir*
Uses of the word *mismo,* Ex. p. 129
Possessive adjectives *(mi, mis; tu, tus,* etc.*)*
  (See also *Grammar Summary*, p. 223)

Unit 10

Pronouns with prepositions *(para mí, conmigo,* etc.*),* Ex. p. 143
Ordinal numbers

Unit 11

Present tense and uses of *pensar, creer,* Ex. p. 157
Expression: *gustar* meaning "to like", Ex: p. 157

Unit 12

Expressions describing the weather, Ex. p. 171

Unit 13

Reflexive verbs *(levantarse,* etc.*),* Ex. p. 185
Present tense of *salir,* Ex. p. 185

Unit 14
Future tense, Ex. p. 199

Unit 15
Preterite tense, Ex. p. 213

Japanese

Unit 1

The markers *wa/ga, o, no, ni/e, ka, yo*
Forms and placement of verbs in the sentence
Use of *-kute*
Honorific suffixes and verb forms
Formulas for greeting, leave taking, and making someone's acquaintance
Forms of nouns and pronouns
Adjectives, e.g., *samui*, and adjectival nouns, e.g., *hontoo*
 (See also Unit 11)
The verb *desu*
Overview of *kanji, hiragana,* and *katakana*

Unit 2

The suffixes *-chan* and *-sai*
The verb suffix *-te*
Some characteristics of feminine speech
Superlatives with *ichiban*
Cardinal numbers
Omission of words
The markers *ga, ni, de, kara* (from), and *made*
Use of pronouns
Negative of *desu*

Unit 3

The markers *mo, to, kara* (because)
demo...ka ne to prompt negotiation
 (See also Unit 10)
Comparisons and preferences with *hoo*
Making suggestions with *-oo ka*
The softening question marker *kashira*
Degrees of politeness
Counters: people, classic, age, days of the week

Unit 4

Counters: hotel stay, time
The marker *to* (if/when)
Marking finality with *-tte shimau*
  (See also Unit 9)
Fractions
Ordinal numbers

Unit 5

Directives with *-te kudasai*
The marker *no* in feminine speech
Obligation with *-nai to ikemasen*
The ending *-tara* (when/if)
Reported speech marked with *tte*
  (See also Unit 9)
Counters: building floors, weeks
Ordinal numbers
The marker *de* (by means of)
Polite softening with *ga* and *keredomo*

Unit 6

Counters: minutes, elapsed hours
Months of the year
Days of the month
Markers: *dake, ni* (specific time words)
  (See also Unit 9)
The ending *-tari* for verbs in random series
Intention with *tsumori (desu)*

Unit 7

toka...toka for either...or
Modifying a noun with a verb or verb phrase (e.g., *ni nomu kusuri*)
  (See also Unit 12)
Counters: flat objects, elapsed months
The verb ending *-temo* with and without *daijoobu/ii(n) desu*
Comparison with *yori*

Unit 8

Markers *ni* (benefit), *yoo* (purpose), *no*
The adjective suffix *-te*
Suggestions with the verb suffix *-oo*

Irregular and regular verb forms
Expressing ability with *-emasu/-raremasu*

Unit 9

Reported speech marked with *tte*
  (See also Unit 5)
Markers: *no yo* and sentence-final *wa* in feminine speech, *-de* (location; vs. *ni*), *ya* vs. *to*
Emphasis with *moo*
Softening with *-te*
Marking finality with *-tte shimau*
Expressing "only" with either *shika* or *dake*
  (See also Unit 6)
Expressions with *-te miru*
Some uses of *to omou*

Unit 10

Informal and honorific usages among women
demo...ka to prompt negotiation
  (See also Unit 3)
Marking finality with *-chattan desu*
Adjective inflection: *-soo*
Verb inflections: future intention, past, negative, negative past, "let's..."

Unit 11

Polite requests with *kudasaimasen ka*
Past and negative adjective endings

Unit 12

Expressing excesses with adjective forms plus *sugimasu*
Modifying a noun with a verb or verb phrase (e.g., *mainichi kuru hito*)
  (See also Unit 7)

Unit 13

Inflecting and noninflecting adjectives to express "to become" (with *naru*)
Making nouns of verbs with *no/wa*

Unit 14

The pattern *ko-so-a-do* for distance from speaker
Intention with *-oo to omoimasu*
Asking and giving permission with *-te mo ii desu*
"Plain past" with *-ta*

Unit 15

Causative with *-te-morau*
When-clauses with *toki*
The suffixes *-go* and *-jin*

Russian

Unit 1

Polite versus familiar forms in verbs
Gender in adjectives
Gender in nouns

Unit 2

Polite versus familiar forms in pronouns
Present tense forms of verbs
   (See also Unit 9)
Gender in pronouns
Prepositional case with *B*, Ex. pp. 31–32
   (See also Unit 5, Unit 8, and *Grammar Summary*, p. 211)

Unit 3

Expressions with *HA*
   (See also Unit 5)
Expressions of possession with *y*
   (See also Unit 4, Unit 12)
Accusative case of nouns, Ex. p. 44
   (See also *Grammar Summary*, p. 211)

Unit 4

Dative case of pronouns
   (See also Unit 10 and *Grammar Summary*, p. 212)
Expressions of possession with *y*
   (See also Unit 3, Unit 12)
Instrumental case with *c*
   (See also *Grammar Summary*, p. 211)

Unit 5

Prepositional case with *B*
   (See also Unit 2, Unit 8, and *Grammar Summary*, p. 211)
Expressions with *HA*
   (See also Unit 3)

В versus *НА* for 'for'
Some comparative adjectives
Plural forms of nouns, Ex. p. 70

Unit 6

Forms and usage of genitive nouns
   (See also Unit 12 and *Grammar Summary*, p. 211)
Forms of nouns with number words
Forms of nouns with *НЕТ*
Nominative and accusative adjective endings, Ex. p. 81

Unit 7

Forms of *ВАС* with numbers
В in time expressions
'from . . . to' with numbers
В and *НА* with *ХОДИ́ТЬ*
Time of day
Ordinal numbers to 12th

Unit 8

Ordinal numbers beyond 12th
Accusative and genitive cases after prepositions, Ex. p. 105
   (See also *Grammar Summary*, p. 211)

Unit 9

С with genitive
Present tense forms of regular verbs in -*АТЬ*, -*ЕТЬ*, -*ИТЬ*, Ex. p. 119
   (See also *Grammar Summary*, p. 212)

Unit 10

Genitive case after *МНО́ГО*
ЗА for 'for'
Dative case of pronouns, Ex. p. 131
   (See also *Grammar Summary*, p. 212)

Unit 11

Forms and usage of *ЛЮБИ́ТЬ*
Verbal prefixes
   (See also Unit 14)
Past tense of verbs, Ex. p. 143
   (See also *Grammar Summary*, p. 212)

Unit 12

Expressions of possession with *у*
  (See also Unit 3, Unit 4)
Forms and usage of dative nouns, Ex. p. 159
  (See also *Grammar Summary*, p. 211)
Forms and usage of genitive nouns
  (See also Unit 6 and *Grammar Summary*, p. 211)
ПО with dative case
Superlative adjectives
Adverbial expressions (e.g., *ТЕПЛО́*)
Impersonal expressions, Ex. p. 159

Unit 13

Verbs taking certain cases, Ex. p. 174
Verbs ending in -*СЯ*, Ex. p. 174
Genitive case after *МА́ЛО*
Dative case to express age
  (See also *Grammar Summary*, p. 211)
  ГО́ДА/ЛЕТ in expressions of age
Genitive case after *ПО́СЛЕ*
Present and past tense forms of *ЖИТЬ*
Case endings on relative pronouns

Unit 14

Verbal prefixes
  (See also Unit 11)
Future tense forms of verbs, Ex. p. 190
  (See also *Grammar Summary*, p. 213)
Adverbial expressions for times of day (e.g., *ДНЁМ*)
Present tense forms of *УЧИ́ТЬСЯ*
Forms and usage of perfective verbs, Ex. p. 190
  (See also Unit 15 and *Grammar Summary*, p. 213)
Instrumental case with verbs such as *СТАТЬ*
Pronoun forms with *С*
Forms and usage of *ПОЙТИ́*

Unit 15

The particle *Же*
Case endings on personal names
Forms and usage of perfective verbs
  (See also Unit 14 and *Grammar Summary*, p. 213)
The verbal prefixes -*ПРИ* and -*у*

Pronoun forms with *O*
  (See also *Grammar Summary*, p. 211)
Impersonal expressions
  (See also Unit 12)
Time expressions with days of the week
Genitive case after *ИЗ*
Verbs of motion, Ex. p. 206
  (See also *Grammar Summary*, p. 213)

Greek

Unit 1

Polite versus familiar forms
  (See also Unit 3 and Unit 12)
Negation of verbs
  (See also Unit 3 and Unit 15)
Adjective-noun agreement, Ex. p. 17
  (See also Unit 4 and *Grammar Summary*, p. 224)
Present tense of verbs
  (See also Unit 2 and *Grammar Summary*, p. 223)
Present tense forms of *ime* (I am), Ex. p. 17

Unit 2

Gender of nouns
Present tense forms of *eho* (I have), Ex. p. 31
Present tense forms of *doulevo* (I work)
  (See also Unit 11)
Present tense of verbs
  (See also Unit 1 and *Grammar Summary*, p. 223)

Unit 3

Polite versus familiar forms
  (See also Unit 1 and Unit 12)
na to link verbs
  (See also Unit 4 and Unit 5)
Future tense
  (See also Unit 5 and Unit 15)
The diminutive ending *-aki*
  (See also Unit 7)
Question formation with question words
Negation of verbs
  (See also Unit 1 and Unit 15), Ex. p. 45
Present tense forms of *thelo* (I want)
  (See also Unit 11)

Unit 4

Usage of *ine* (there is/are)
na to link verbs
   (See also Unit 3 and Unit 5)
na meaning 'here'
ti(n) for *i* after *me*
   (See also Unit 10)
Adjective-noun agreement
   (See also Unit 1 and *Grammar Summary*, p. 224)
Forms and usage of definite and indefinite articles
   (See also *Grammar Summary*, pp. 223–24)
Present tense forms of *boró* (I can)

Unit 5

ti(n) for *i* after *yiá*
   (See also Unit 10)
na to link verbs
   (See also Unit 3 and Unit 4)
Future tense
   (See also Unit 3 and Unit 15)
Plural of nouns, Ex. p. 73
Present tense forms of *pao* (I go)

Unit 6

Comparative of adjectives with *-tero*
Expressions of time, Ex. p. 87
Present tense forms of *fevgo, anigo, klino* (I leave, I open, I close)

Unit 7

Quantity expressions of the form *ena koutí spirta, ena potiri neró*
The diminutive ending *-aki*
   (See also Unit 3)
Forms and placement of adjectives, Ex. p. 101
Present tense forms of *protimó, kitó, miló, pernó* (I prefer, I look, I speak, I pass)
   (See also Unit 11)

Unit 8

Comparative of adjectives with *pió*, Ex. p. 115
Usage of *aresi*
   (See also Unit 11)
Present tense forms of *dino* (I give)
   (See also Unit 11)

Unit 9

Plural of neuter nouns in -*a*
Usage of *toso* (so)
ti(n) for *i* after *apó*
  (See also Unit 10)
Forms and usage of possessive pronouns
  (See also *Grammar Summary*, p. 224), Ex. p. 129
Present tense forms of *klino* (I shut)
  (See also Unit 11)

Unit 10

Gender forms of the indefinite article
  (See also *Grammar Summary*, p. 224)
Forms of pronouns after *yiá*
The diminutive endings -*itsa* and -*oula*
Forms of the definite article after prepositions, Ex. p. 143
Present tense forms of *pino* (I drink)
  (See also Unit 11)

Unit 11

Forms and usage of *aresi*
The two regular patterns of present tense verbs
  (See also *Grammar Summary*, p. 223), Ex. p. 155

Unit 12

Polite versus familiar forms
Present tense forms of *érhoume, leo, tro* (I come, I say, I eat), Ex. p. 169

Unit 13

Past tense forms of regular verbs
  (See also *Grammar Summary*, p. 223)

Unit 14

Past tense patterns of several irregular verbs, Ex. p. 197

Unit 15

Various uses of *na*
Positive and negative future tense formation
  (See also *Grammar Summary*, p. 223), Ex. p. 209

Arabic

Unit 1

Number
   (See also Unit 4)
'Yes' and 'no'
Gender in nouns and verbs, Ex. p. 9, p. 13
   (See also Unit 3 and Unit 4)
Dual number in nouns
   (See also Unit 2)
9ind- to show possession
   (See also Unit 3 and *Grammar Summary*, p. 218)
Polite religious formulas
Omission of 'to be'
   (See also Unit 3)
Statements vs. questions
Forms and uses of the definite article, Ex. p. 17
   (See also *Grammar Summary*, p. 217)
Arabic names and regional usages
Basic letter forms

Unit 2

Adjective forms and usage
   (See also *Grammar Summary*, p. 217)
Pronoun agreement with antecedent
Noun-adjective phrases, Ex. p. 31
Dual number in nouns, Ex. p. 31
   (See also Unit 1)
the letters *baa* and *alif*

Unit 3

Gender in verbs
   (See also Unit 1, Unit 4)
9ind- to show possession
   (See also Unit 1 and *Grammar Summary*, p. 218)
Commands
   (See also *Grammar Summary*, p. 219)
Pronominal noun endings
   (See also *Grammar Summary*, p. 218)
Non-past verb forms, Ex. pp. 43, 44
   (See also *Grammar Summary*, p. 219)
Subject pronouns
   (See also *Grammar Summary*, p. 220)
Numbers used with nouns
The letters *lam* and *taa*

Unit 4

Adjective plurals
  (See also *Grammar Summary*, p. 217)
Verb gender, Ex. p. 58
  (See also Unit 1, Unit 3)
Numbers, Ex. p. 53
  (See also Unit 1)
'abilla with non-past verbs
Noun "constructs" and possessives, Ex. p. 55
  (See also Unit 5 and *Grammar Summary*, p. 218)
B-prefix in verbs, Ex. p. 57
  (See also Unit 5, Unit 14)
Modal verb usage, Ex. p. 57
  (See also Unit 5)
Verb negation
  (See also Unit 7 and *Grammar Summary*, p. 221)
The letter *yaa*

Unit 5

Forms of address
Objective pronouns
  (See also *Grammar Summary*, p. 220)
Modal verb usage
  (See also Unit 4)
Possession with *taba9*
  (See also *Grammar Summary*, p. 218)
B-prefix in verbs
  (See also Unit 4, Unit 14)
Noun "constructs," Ex. p. 73
  (See also Unit 4)
Ordinal numbers
The letters *waaw* and *nuun*

Unit 6

Number genders
B-prefix forms of *kaan*
Sound plurals of nouns
  (See also *Grammar Summary*, p. 217)
Broken plurals of nouns
  (See also Unit 7 and *Grammar Summary*, p. 217)

Unit 7

Singular nouns with quantities
Non-past verb forms of "weak" verbs
   (See also Unit 12 and *Grammar Summary*, p. 219)
Verb negation
   (See also Unit 4 and *Grammar Summary*, p. 221)
Negation of *9ind-* and *fii*
   (See also *Grammar Summary*, pp. 217, 221)
Broken plurals with *-aw-*
   (See also Unit 6)
Adjective agreement in money amounts
The letters *siin, shiin,* and *-a*

Unit 8

Syntax with *haada*
Comparative adjectives, Ex. p. 115
   (See also *Grammar Summary*, p. 217)
Adjective agreement, Ex. p. 115
   (See also *Grammar Summary*, p. 217)
Pronoun endings and *yyaa-*
The letters *kaaf* and *daal*
Writing doubled consonants

Unit 9

Consonant patterns in word roots
Active verb participles, Ex. p. 129
   (See also Unit 10 and *Grammar Summary*, p. 220)
"Relative" derived adjectives
The letter *9ayn*

Unit 10

Passive participle forms and uses, Ex. p. 142
   (See also *Grammar Summary*, p. 220)
Active participles of derived verbs, Ex. p. 142
   (See also Unit 9 and *Grammar Summary*, p. 220)
Use of *illi*
   (See also Unit 12)
The letters *Taa, faa,* and *qaaf*

Unit 11

Use of *innuh*
Gender endings on participles

9am with non-past verbs
Feminine singular agreement with *naas*
Past tense forms of regular and "hollow" verbs, Ex. p. 157
   (See also *Grammar Summary*, p. 218)
The letters *ghayn* and *jiim*

Unit 12

Use of *illi*
   (See also Unit 10)
Past tense of "weak" verbs
   (See also Unit 7 and *Grammar Summary*, p. 218)
The irregular verb *aja*
The letters *xaa, dhaal,* and *DHaa*

Unit 13

9a, 9ala after *raaH*
Command form of verbs, Ex. p. 183
   (See also *Grammar Summary*, p. 219)
Verbal noun patterns, Ex. p. 183
The letters *Haa, haa, Saad,* and *-aa*

Unit 14

B-prefix in verbs
   (See also Unit 4, Unit 5)
rah to indicate future time, Ex. p. 197
The letters *Daad, thaa,* and *hamza*

Unit 15

Verb strings, Ex. p. 211
Script styles

Appendix III: A Catalogue and Description of the Comprehension Exercises According to Level of Skill Involved

Notes:
The purpose of this Appendix is to provide you with a rapid review of all the exercises of any given category that are available in your book. Since the nature of each category has already been characterized and illustrated in "A Gradated Program for Increasing Levels of Skill," the description of the exercise is generally as brief as possible while still giving some idea of subject matter involved.

Since this listing also includes the exercises from the *Read and Understand* and the *Revision/Review* section of your book, you will note that some are done on the basis of written material alone, i.e., with no tape provided. (It may be helpful, however, to introduce a new type of exercise whenever possible by selecting first from those that can be done without a tape, since this is usually an easier form of activity that can build the students' confidence.) Unless the words "no tape" are included in the listing to follow, you can assume that the exercise depends on a dialogue from your cassettes.

The reference following each entry below (e.g., 1/14/3) is to the unit number, the page number, and the number of the exercise on that page. When answers are supplied with an exercise, you will find the page number where they are located indicated after the instructions.

French

Dictation
write out numbers read on tape	1/	16/	4
	2/	29/	1
	4/	57/	3

Rearranging the text
a customer and a baker *(no tape)*	7/	99/	2
	10/	141/	2

True/False
ordering a meal	10/	142/	4
renting an apartment	13/	182/	3

Multiple Choice
information about participants in a dialogue	2/	30/	3
a visit to a tourist office	5/	71/	1
purchases at a pharmacy	8/	114/	3
ordering a meal	10/	142/	4

Checking Off Items

items ordered at a café	3/	43/	1
items ordered for a picnic	7/	100/	3
a meal ordered from a menu	10/	140/	1
pictures of things liked and disliked by speaker	1/	155/	1

Fill-ins

members of a family tree according to dialogue *(no tape)*	2/	30/	4
the number of various food items ordered for an outing	3/	44/	3
names of rooms described on floor plan of a house	13/	181/	1
price of items on snack bar poster, as described on tape	10/	142/	3
clock faces with times spoken on tape	6/	85/	2

Grids

fill in likes, dislikes, and intense dislikes of speaker	1/	156/	2

Matchings

(no tape provided)

information for a hotel registration form	1/	15/	1
phrases indicated with missing parts of a conversation between a waiter and a customer	1/	16/	3
professions listed with drawings of people at work	2/	29/	2
phrases with missing parts of a conversation between a motorist and employee at the tourist office	5/	71/	2
pictures with sentences describing them	8/	113/	1
phrases with missing parts of a letter	12/	167/	1
	12/	196/	3
phrases with missing parts of the description of a road accident	15/	207/	2

(corroborated by tape)

phrases with missing parts of a conversation between a hotel clerk and a guest	4/	58/	4
as above, but regarding purchase of train tickets	9/	128/	3
phrases with missing parts of description of Paris	11/	156/	3

as above, but regarding rooms in a house	13/ 182/	4
phrases with missing parts of a dialogue concerning an outing to the beach	14/ 194/	1

Answering Informational Questions in English

passages from a tourist brochure *(no tape)*	12/ 170/	1
a letter from a friend *(no tape)*	14/ 198/	—
what a couple orders at a restaurant	3/ 44/	4
days of the week various activities take place on	6/ 85/	1
people planning a vacation	6/ 86/	4
a conversation at a tobacco shop	7/ 99/	1
a shopping expedition	8/ 114/	2
purchasing a train ticket	9/ 127/	2
a letter from a friend	12/ 167/	2
description of a seaside town	12/ 168/	3
description of a vacation	15/ 207/	1
a disastrous journey	15/ 208/	3

Translating

translate the following dates *(no tape)*	6/ 86/	3

Answering Informational Questions in French

write out answers to math problems *(no tape)*	1/ 16/	3
answer questions as to your activities tomorrow	14/ 195/	2
answer questions put to you, and take part in a conversation	14/ 200/	1-3

Miscellaneous

identify from the inflection of the voice whether the words spoken are a statement or a question	4/ 57/	3
follow directions on a map according to the tape; see where you end up	5/ 72/	3

German

True/False

understanding the letterhead on hotel stationery *(no tape)*	3/	46/	1
understanding a museum schedule *(no tape)*	6/	88/	2
announcements of supermarket items on sale *(no tape)*	7/	102/	—
a woman describes herself and her city *(no tape)*	Rev./	220/	—
an advertisement for a department store	8/	112/	3
an interview with two little boys	2/	30/	3
a travel agent describes fares	9/	128/	5
a conversation at an art exhibit	11/	154/	2
plans for the weekend	15/	211/	1

Multiple Choice

identifying professions based on drawings *(no tape)*	4/	60/	1
reading a weather forecast *(no tape)*	12/	172/	1
advertisment for a vacation resort *(no tape)*	12/	172/	2
understanding a horoscope *(no tape)*	15/	214/	—
a pharmacist's directions for medication	8/	114/	5
ordering at a restaurant	10/	139/	2
a man describes his likes and dislikes	11/	154/	1
a radio advertisment for Switzerland	12/	170/	2
a woman describes her lifestyle and hobbies	13/	182/	1
people describe their vacations	14/	197/	2
a man describes his work and vacation	6/	85/	3
the selection of a good restaurant	10/	139/	1

Checking Off Items

telephone numbers mentioned on tape	2/	29/	2
local sights to see	6/	85/	2
items ordered from a menu (add up the check)	10/140 −1/		3,4
tourist attractions in East and West Berlin	12/	169/	1

Fill-ins

price labels on fruits described	7/	100/	3
prices of items described at the supermarket	8/	111/	1
fill in a registration form according to instructions	1/	16/	3
room numbers and their rates at a hotel	3/	44/	3
prices described of items on a menu (add up the check)	4/	58/	2
items ordered at a café	4/	58/	3
the time of day, as recited on tape	6/	85/	1
train departures and travel times	6/	86/	4, 5
items ordered at a restaurant (add up the check)	10/	141/	4
activities in a man's daily routine	13/	183/	2

Grids

fill in the time of day for people listed, according to their greetings	1/	15/	1
room numbers and hotel guests	2/	29/	1
hotel accommodations sought by a man and woman	3/	43/	1
people and the amounts of money they exchange at a bank	3/	43/	2
information for train schedules	9/	127/	2
	9/	128/	4
people and their future plans	15/	212/	3

Matchings

(no tape provided)

people with hotel accommodations preferred	3/	46/	2
clock faces to written forms for time of day	6/	88/	1
match up ideal partners from newspaper "lonely hearts" ads	13/	186/	1
verbs listed with blanks in descriptions of a man's day	Rev./	221/	—

(tape optional)

phrases with blanks related to pictures of people	1/	15/	2
answers to questions asked of a tourist	2/	30/	4
	11/	155/	4
phrases with blanks in a conversation about a vacation	13/	183/	3
	14/	196/	1

68   Just Listen 'n Learn Language Programs

(tape essential)

countries listed to pictures of people who describe themselves on tape	1/	16/	4
answers to questions from dialogue regarding prices of stamps at post office	7/	99/	2
phrases with blanks in train announcements	9/	127/	3
pictures of activities described on tape with days listed in a person's diary	14/	198/	4
names of train stops listed with blanks ordered "a" through "f," according sequence of announcements on tape	5/	71/	2
street diagrams with descriptions of routes to various places	5/	72/	3
items on a shopping list to their weights and measurements	8/	112/	2
areas indicated on a map with blanks ordered "a" through "d," according to the sequence in which described on tape	11/	155/	3

Answering Informational Questions In English

understanding speaking captions in drawings *(no tape)*	1/	18/	1
a description of a woman and her family *(no tape)*	2/	32/	1
understanding a tourist brochure *(no tape)*	5/	74/	—
an advertisment for clothing *(no tape)*	8/	116/	—
signs at a train station *(no tape)*	9/	130/	1
a train schedule *(no tape)*	1/	130/	2
descriptions of restaurants *(no tape)*	10/	144/	—
a postcard from a friend *(no tape)*	11/	157/	—
a letter from parents to their daughter *(no tape)*	14/	200/	—
prices of items at an art gallery	7/	99/	1
announcements at a train station	9/	126/	1
a dissatisfied customer at a restaurant	10/	142/	5
a weather forecast	12/	170/	4
people describe their vacations	14/	197/	2
a man invites a woman to the theater	15/	212/	4

Supplying Missing Parts of a Conversation

fill in the caption blanks in a dialogue between a woman and an employee at a clothing store	8/	113/	4

Answering Informational Questions in German

pretending you are a reporter, take notes by filling in answers to the following questions based on a taped interview	12/	170/	3
questions about a woman interviewed following her vacation (this exercise is also part of a crossword puzzle)	13/	184/	4
fill in a young woman's diary according to the activities she describes	15/	211/	2

Miscellaneous

listen to the inflection of the voices on tape and indicate whether what you hear is a question or a command	5/	71/	1
following the map in the book according to the taped instructions, indicate where you end up	5/	72/	4
word puzzles and guessing games	1/	18/	2
	4/	60/	2
	7/	100/	4
	13/	184/	4
	13/	186/	2
	Rev./	218/	1

Italian

Rearranging the Text

dialogue between a doctor and a patient *(tape corroborates)*	14/	198/	3
a tourist asks directions at a bus stop *(tape corroborates)*	6/	85/	4

True/False

locations pictured on a map *(no tape)*	5/	72/	5
museum schedules	6/	84/	2
Italian newspapers	7/	99/	2

Multiple Choice

understanding a hotel receipt *(no tape)*	4/	60/	—
understanding a recipe *(no tape)*	8/	116/	—
understanding a wine label *(no tape)*	10/	144/	—
understanding a restaurant check *(no tape)*	11/	158/	—
a weather forecast *(no tape)*	12/	169/	1
speakers who introduce themselves	1/	14/	2
a speaker and a passerby	1/	15/	3
employees unable to provide certain accommodations	3/	44/	3
three dialogues of a tourist asking information	5/	71/	1-3
items in a grocery store	8/	113/	1
two dialogues about asking for travel information	9/	125/	1, 2
a speaker describes his early life	13/	182/	1
a man tells of the languages he knows	13/	183/	3
what a couple orders at a restaurant	10/	141/	1, 2
two youths make a date	14/	197/	1
a chat between friends	15/	210/	1

Checking Off Items

check on the menu the items ordered at a restaurant	10/	142/	4
as above, but with two people ordering	11/	153/	1, 2
a baker describes types of bread	7/	99/	1

Fill-ins

write in the date for the day described *(no tape)*	13/	183/	4
write in weights on baggage tags	2/	29/	3
phone numbers of hotels	2/	29/	5
fill in price tags for items described	7/	100/	3
identify items at a grocer's, as described	8/	114/	4

Grids

trains and their track numbers *(no tape)*	2/	28/	1, 2
airline flights and their destinations	2/	29/	4
types of coffee brands, their weights and prices	8/	113/	2

Matchings

(no tape provided)

directions indicated with locations on a map	5/	72/	4
blanks in sentences with "third person phrases" (such as *bisogna . . .*")	9/	127/	1
descriptions with types of food	10/	142/	3
hotel rooms with their locations	11/	154/	3
adjectives with types of food and drink	11/	154/	4
answers with questions on subject of food	4/	58/	3
expressions for weather with pictures	12/	170/	3
phrases with blanks in dialogue regarding recreational activities	14/	198/	4

(tape merely corroborates)

people with their professions	3/	43/	1
questions with answers regarding buying a train ticket	9/	126/	3
greetings to be used with people pictured	1/	15/	3
blanks in sentences with expressions of courtesy	7/	100/	4
phrases with blanks in dialogue at a pharmacy	8/	114/	3
phrases with blanks in dialogue about automotive needs	12/	169/	2
verbs with blanks in a conversation	15/	210/	2
match up two parts of a conversation	3/	44/	5

(tape essential)

who comes from where?	1/	14/	1
hotel guests with their room numbers	3/	43/	3
hotels with their prices	4/	57/	1
who orders what at a restaurant	4/	57/	2
clock faces with times of day spoken on tape	6/	84/	1
activities described with days of the week	6/	85/	3
announcements of movies, etc., to preferences expressed by speakers on tape	14/	197/	2

Answering Informational Questions in English

understanding a flight schedule at the airport *(no tape)*	2/ 32/	—
understanding a train ticket *(no tape)*	9/ 130/	—
a guidebook describing monuments *(no tape)*	13/ 186/	—
a movie guide *(no tape)*	14/ 200/	—
a short poem on the months of the year	12/ 170/	—

Translating

translate the English phrases provided and write a postcard similar to the model *(no tape)*	15/ 211/	13

Reenacting a Dialogue

after hearing a tape of people describing their pasts, answer similar questions put to you	13/ 182/	2

Miscellaneous

fill in a hotel registration form and answer questions *(no tape)*	3/ 46/	—
crossword puzzle	9/ 126/	4

Spanish

Dictation

pretending you are a waiter, take down the items ordered	10/ 142/	3

Rearranging the text

(corroborated by tapes)

a conversation between friends	1/ 15/	1
looking for a campsite	3/ 44/	5
getting information at a train station	6/ 85/	2
hailing a taxi	9/ 127/	1

True /False

location of items in a department store *(no tape)*	2/ 32/	—
questions from a newspaper story *(no tape)*	15/ 214/	—
facts about people in dialogue	1/ 16/	4
locations of places in Spain	2/ 29/	1
location of places described on map provided	5/ 70/	1
distances between places on map, as described on tape	3/ 72/	4

Multiple Choice

newspaper ad for apartments to rent *(no tape)*	3/ 46/	—
announcements of train departures *(no tape)*	9/ 130/	—
the Canary Islands and the Balearic Islands *(no tape)*	7/ 102/	—
questions about the Costa del Sol *(no tape)*	11/ 158/	—
indicate how much change you are given from various stores	4/ 57/	3
questions regarding a weather forecast	12/ 169/	1
questions from a news bulletin	14/ 196/	1

Checking Off Items

circle objects on a table as mentioned on tape	3/ 43/	1
check off accommodations in a hotel guest's room	3/ 43/	2
items on a menu as ordered by two people	4/ 56/	1
items a customer orders at a department store	8/ 113/	1
as above, but with two people	8/ 113/	2
services a woman requests at the beauty salon	14/ 198/	3
features of apartments described by their renters	3/ 44/	4
items ordered at a grocery store	7/ 98/	1
items liked and disliked by a speaker	11/ 156/	4

Grids

information on train schedules	6/ 86/	4
prices and quantity of items in a department store	7/ 99/	2
people's names, the trains they take, price of tickets, platform number	9/ 128/	4

vacation preferences of various speakers	11/ 156/	3
temperatures for different seasons and months in Spain	12/ 170/	4
fill in and add up the check for each table at a restaurant	4/ 57/	4

Matchings

(no tape provided)

match items to prices on a check, using menu as guide	4/ 60/	—

(tape merely corroborates)

phrases to missing parts of dialogue between waiter and a customer	4/ 58/	5
activities described with the time of day	13/ 183/	2
answers with questions about a young woman's day	13/ 184/	3
phrases to missing parts of conversation about a man's vacation	15/ 211/	1
phrases to missing parts of a dialogue in a restaurant	10/ 142/	4

(tape essential)

names and descriptions of people	2/ 29/	2
people and hotel accommodations desired	3/ 44/	3
names of people to illustrations of directions they have been given	5/ 71/	2
"ratings" for restaurants according to descriptions of them	10/ 141/	1
people and items they have ordered at a restaurant	10/ 141/	2
items of food with their measures of quantity	7/ 99/	3

Answering Informational Questions in English

Questions from a paragraph about various people *(no tape)*	1/ 18/	—
understanding a bus schedule *(no tape)*	6/ 88/	—
	7/ 102/	—
questions about Spanish pharmacies *(no tape)*	8/ 116/	1
listening to tape and studying map provided, write out locations of monuments referred to	5/ 71/	3
questions about a shopping expedition	8/ 114/	3

Supplying Missing Parts of a Conversation

complete dialogue between you and a gas station attendant *(no tape, but based on earlier dialogue)*	9/	128/	3
a customer and a waiter	4/	56/	2
a saleslady and a difficult customer	7/	100/	4

Translating

translate signs at customs authority *(no tape)*	15/	212/	2
translate phrases into Spanish, using tape as model	15/	212/	3

Answering Informational Questions in the Target Languages

answer questions on a hotel bill *(no tape)*	12/	172/	—
ask people their professions, according to the drawings	1/	16/	3

Reenacting a Dialogue

pretend you are at a restaurant, and order the items pictured *(no tape)*	4/	62/	—
answer questions put to you by a customs officer	1/	15/	2

Miscellaneous

fill in an application form for opening a bank account *(no tape)*	8/	116/	2
crossword puzzles *(clues on tape)*	{ 9/ 12/	127/ 170/	2 3

Japanese

True/False

personal information details about a speaker on the tape	2/	/	10

Multiple Choice

statements about speaker's home	13/	/	11
details about speaker's preferences	14/	/	5

Checking Off Items

names of people introduced	1/	/	1
identify greetings heard on tape	1/	/	4

Fill-Ins

details in personal information phrases	2/	/	9
floor counters in building locations	5/	/	5
prepositions and connectors in sentences asking directions	5/	/	7
week counters in a dialogue at a cleaners	5/	/	10
counters for stamps and ham	7/	/	10
dialogue elements of polite mealtime conversation	10/	/	4
weather-word elements for a personal dialogue	12/	/	3
month names in statements about Tokyo weather	12/	/	4
speaker's residence information	13/	/	8
sentence transition words in a passage about plans	14/	/	4

Matchings

dialogue elements in greetings	1/	/	3
weather comments with English translation	1/	/	6
Japanese phrases with pictured situations	1/	/	8
names of days of the week with English translation	2/	/	2
personal conversation elements with responses	2/	/	4
people counters with English translation	2/	/	8
food words with English translation	3/	/	3
money amounts as written with amounts as customarily spoken	3/	/	7
hotel registration phrases with English translation	4/	/	1
hotel registration phrases with English translation	4/	/	5
hotel facility information questions with English translation	4/	/	8

pictures with direction-giving phrases	5/	/	1
halves of sentences giving directions	5/	/	4
pharmaceutical items with their translations	7/	/	7
color words with Japanese translations	8/	/	1
travel words with Japanese translations	9/	/	1
expressions of desire with English translation	9/	/	4
train-travel vocabulary with English translations	9/	/	7
hotel phrases with English translation	9/	/	10
formal with casual expressions	10/	/	7
names of cuisines with English translations	10/	/	10
European country names with English translations	11/	/	1
hotel phrases with English translation	11/	/	7
weather phrases with English translation	12/	/	1
weather phrases with English translation	12/	/	8
time of year with weather per tape statements	12/	/	11
sports words with English translation	13/	/	4
phrases asking where someone lives with English translation	13/	/	7
apartment rental phrases with English translation	13/	/	10
phrases about a trip to a museum with English translation	14/	/	1
public performance phrases with English translation	14/	/	8
short useful phrases with English translation	14/	/	11
sentences about language ability with English translation	15/	/	1
phrases about the day's events with English translation	15/	/	4
requests to change hotel rooms with English translation	15/	/	7

Answering Informational Questions in English

details from a getting-aquainted dialogue	1/	/	9
people's professions from tape dialogues	2/	/	12
details from a mealtime dialogue	3/	/	4
details from a dialogue about a meal	3/	/	8
hotel registration information	4/	/	6
room numbers of hotel guests from tape list	4/	/	9
hotel features from tape description	4/	/	10
details from a dialogue asking directions	5/	/	8
details from a dialogue at a cleaners	5/	/	11

details from a dialogue arranging a date	6/	/	5
details from a dialogue arranging a date	6/	/	8
details from a clerk's tally of items purchased	7/	/	1
details from a recounting of a shopping trip	8/	/	2
details from a tape recounting of health complaints	8/	/	5
details on credit cards accepted from a tape dialogue	8/	/	7
details from a tape dialogue on purchasing a plate	8/	/	8
construct a shopping list from a tape dialogue	8/	/	11
details from a dialogue about a trip to Kyoto	9/	/	2
details from a dialogue about a trip to Akihabara	9/	/	5
details from a dialogue on train travel	9/	/	8
details from a dialogue about a trip to the hot springs	9/	/	11
details in a restaurant dialogue from prompts in Japanese	10/	/	5
details from a dialogue about plans to dine out	10/	/	11
details from a dialogue about someone's love of travel	11/	/	2
details from a dialogue about where speakers' parents live	11/	/	5
details from a dialogue about music preferences	11/	/	11
details from a dialogue about the weather	12/	/	2
details from a dialogue with a visitor to Japan	12/	/	5
details from a dialogue about a speaker's plans	14/	/	2
details from a dialogue about buying theater tickets	14/	/	9
details from a speaker's narration about learning a language	15/	/	2

Translating

hotel registration phrases	4/	/	2
hotel registration information with tape and written prompts	4/	/	7
note gist of train directions from tape	5/	/	2
directions for taking a train to a certain destination	5/	/	3
questions asking directions	5/	/	9
dialogue elements at a cleaners	5/	/	12
times of day	6/	/	2
questions one might ask a tourist	6/	/	12
telephone numbers	7/	/	4
telephone numbers	7/	/	5
a dialogue exchanging addresses and telephone numbers	7/	/	6

elements from a request for directions to a pharmacy	7/	/	8
phrasing requesting specific pharmaceutical items	7/	/	9
questions relating to a post office exchange	7/	/	12
items on a shopping list in a tape dialogue	8/	/	10
sentences of the form _____ *wa* _____ *rashii desu*	11/	/	4

Answering Informational Questions in Japanese

simple personal questions	2/	/	6
hotel registration information	4/	/	3
details from a dialogue arranging to go shopping	6/	/	7
details from a dialogue about arriving in Tokyo	6/	/	10
details from a dialogue about first impressions of Tokyo	6/	/	11
details from a McDonald's lunch order	7/	/	2
details from an exchange at the post office	7/	/	11
details from a dialogue about a trip to Kyoto	9/	/	2
personal questions and details from a tape passage	13/	/	6
details from a dialogue about a rental apartment	13/	/	12

Reenacting a Dialogue

respond to a greeting and introduce oneself	1/	/	2
respond to greetings and small talk	1/	/	5
ask common and personal questions as prompted by tape	2/	/	3
participate in a simple personal conversation	2/	/	5
participate in a simple personal conversation	2/	/	7
talk about your profession	2/	/	13
place a food order using classic counters	3/	/	2
ask people their preferences with tape prompts	3/	/	3
talk about your day touring and your lunch intention	3/	/	5
order dessert for oneself and a friend	3/	/	6
discuss where to have dinner with a friend	3/	/	9
register at a hotel according to tape prompts	4/	/	4
construct questions dealing with time	6/	/	3
make plans with a friend to visit some tourist sites	6/	/	6
negotiate a time to go with a friend to Roppongi	6/	/	9
make simple purchases according to tape prompts	7/	/	3

conduct the purchase of a doll	8/	/	3
purchase medicine for a sore throat	8/	/	6
ask to have a plate delivered to your hotel room	8/	/	9
conduct the purchase of tickets for a sightseeing trip	9/	/	3
construct questions about getting to Akihabara	9/	/	6
conduct purchase of train tickets to Hiroshima	9/	/	9
make arrangements for a trip to a hot spring	9/	/	12
practice polite social phrases of invited guests in a home	10/	/	2
practice polite social phrases of guests away from home	10/	/	3
conduct a room service order from tape prompts	10/	/	6
ask informational questions about a restaurant display	10/	/	9
arrange to meet a friend for dinner	10/	/	12
express likes and dislikes following tape prompts	11/	/	3
give a general invitation to a friend to call	11/	/	6
describe the hotel where you are staying	11/	/	9
talk about your interests	11/	/	12
construct elements of a polite conversation with a visitor	12/	/	6
talk about weather in one's own country	12/	/	12
talk about your home with tape prompts	13/	/	9
invite a friend to Ueno	14/	/	3
invite a friend to see Kabuki	14/	/	10
arrange a trip to Hong Kong	14/	/	13
participate in a conversation about learning a language	15/	/	3
request a larger hotel room	15/	/	8

Miscellaneous

identify spoken phrases as questions or statements	1/	/	7
arrange *romaji* numbers in numerical order	2/	/	1
repeat classic counters following tape model	3/	/	1
draw diagram to correspond to directions given on tape	5/	/	6
repeat minute counters after tape model	6/	/	1
identify social markedness of certain phrases	6/	/	4
pattern drill with ailments and body parts	8/	/	4
make a shopping list for a picnic	8/	/	12
recall polite social phrases of mealtimes	10/	/	1

practice constructing negatives of given adjectives	11/	/	8
insert *deshoo, ne* at the end of provided sentences	11/	/	10
repeat Japanese weather words after the tape	12/	/	9
construct weather phrases using tape and written prompts	12/	/	9
construct phrases of the form _____ *–sugimasu*	12/	/	10
repeat phrases related to sports activities after the tape	13/	/	5
practice demonstrative/interrogative sets	14/	/	6
build sentences with demonstratives and interrogatives	14/	/	7
repeat short useful phrases after a tape	14/	/	12
practice family end-of-day greetings with tape prompts	15/	/	5
practice personal-reaction phrases with tape prompts	15/	/	6
practice phrases to request a larger hotel room	15/	/	9
identify tense of given sentences	15/	/	10
practice past tense forms	15/	/	11
convert given phrases to present and conversational style	15/	/	12

Russian
Rearranging the Text

scrambled dialogue on weekly activities *(no tape)*	7/	94/	8
statements about new acquaintances per dialogue	15/	203/	8

True/False *(from dialogues)*

speakers' personal information	2/	23/	1
speakers' restaurant orders	4/	49/	1
book and newspaper availability	5/	63/	3
restaurant reservation details	10/	127/	5

Multiple Choice *(from dialogues)*

restaurant orders	4/	51/	4
directions to various places	8/	103/	5
statements about speakers' vacations	12/	15/	5
speaker's favorite pastimes	13/	166/	1
speaker's living accommodations and plans	14/	183/	3

Checking Off Items *(from dialogues)*

shopping list of items that are available	6/	79/	5
available seats on airplanes	9/	115/	6

Fill-Ins *(from dialogues)*

speakers' family information	2/	23/	2
numbers in a list	2/	27/	6
floor numbers on which hotel facilities are located	3/	37/	2
amounts spent by speakers at a post office	5/	61/	1
numbers of tickets to various performances	5/	63/	4
grocery items *(per dialogue and pictures)*	5/	66/	6
flower prices on pictured sellers	6/	77/	3
pictured dialogue characters with their illnesses	6/	79/	6
order in which given times appear	7/	87/	1
waiting time for customers	7/	89/	4
vacation schedules for family members	7/	91/	5
train times and platforms	9/	113/	4
key words in a car rental context	9/	117/	8
details in a restaurant order	10/	125/	2
details in a restaurant reservation context	10/	127/	4
restaurant orders	10/	129/	7
restaurant orders *(per dialogue and menu)*	10/	129/	8
superlative adjectives in a sightseeing context	12/	151/	3
details in a passage about vacations	12/	157/	7
details of speakers' vacations	15/	201/	6

Grids *(from dialogues)*

room information on hotel registration forms	3/	39/	3
currencies and amounts on exchange forms	3/	41/	5
address information on postcards	5/	61/	2

Matchings *(from dialogues)*

pictures with speakers' statements	1/	9/	1
	1/	11/	2
nationalities with speakers	1/	13/	3

professions with speakers	1/	13/	4
people with professions	2/	25/	3
people with work locations	2/	25/	4
names with residences	2/	27/	5
names with room numbers	3/	37/	1
people with drink orders	4/	49/	2
restaurant dishes with prices	4/	54/	6
meals with restaurants serving them	4/	54/	7
descriptive adjectives with merchandise	6/	77/	4
shop signs with business hours	7/	89/	3
public transportation stops with destinations	8/	101/	3
Moscow train stations with destinations	9/	111/	1
restaurant dishes with nationalities	10/	125/	1
people's names with likes and dislikes	11/	137/	1
speakers' favorite cities with reasons	11/	141/	6
pen pals on the basis of similar likes	11/	144/	9
speakers with their tours of Moscow	12/	149/	1
cities with their tourist sites	12/	151/	2
pictures with weather forecasts	12/	154/	4
speakers with favorite sports	13/	167/	2
family pictures with speakers' descriptions	13/	169/	4
daily routine details with speakers	13/	169/	5
written with spoken apartment descriptions	13/	171/	7
speakers' training with their professions	14/	185/	6
tourist sites with features of interest	15/	197/	2
written paper titles with spoken descriptions	15/	199/	4
newspaper titles with day of release	15/	199/	5
languages with speaker's ability to speak and read them	15/	203/	9
(no tape provided)			
shops with items for sale	6/	82/	9
business hours on signs with a diary	7/	94/	7
restaurants per menus and food preferences	10/	132/	11
postcard pictures with related messages	12/	160/	10
professions with pictures	14/	185/	5
pictures with plans for 1 million rubles	14/	191/	12

Answering Informational Questions in English

speakers' residences per dialogue	11/	141/	5

Translating

directions to various places	8/	99/	2
type of tickets requested by dialogue speakers	9/	113/	3

Reenacting a Dialogue *(with tape prompts)*

give personal information	2/	27/	7
register at a hotel	3/	39/	4
request a currency exchange	3/	41/	6
ask what there is for breakfast	4/	49/	3
order a meal at a restaurant	4/	51/	5
settle a restaurant bill	4/	54/	8
purchase tickets to the Bolshoi	5/	63/	5
purchase vegetables	5/	66/	8
buy a present for a woman friend	6/	75/	2
ask the time of day	7/	87/	2
talk about your week as a student	7/	91/	6
excuse your way to a bus exit	8/	103/	6
ask directions to the correct train	9/	111/	2
request train information	9/	113/	5
buy airplane tickets	9/	115/	7
ask about renting a car	9/	117/	9
order a light meal	10/	125/	3
make a restaurant reservation	10/	127/	6
order a meal *(per tape prompts and menu)*	10/	129/	9
talk about your likes and dislikes	11/	137/	2
ask questions about Moscow weather	12/	155/	6
talk about your interests	13/	167/	3
talk about your vacation plans	14/	181/	2
talk about an apartment you want	14/	183/	4
talk about your job and plans	14/	185/	7
respond to a theater invitation	14/	187/	9

talk about your artistic interests	15/	197/	3
describe your vacation	15/	201/	7

Miscellaneous

note mistakes in a grocery list per dialogue	5/	66/	7
note mistakes in summary statements per dialogue	6/	75/	1
note which desired purchases are for sale *(no tape)*	6/	82/	8
follow directions on tape to locate sites on a map	8/	99/	1
locate subway stops on a map per tape directions	8/	101/	4
mark a map route per written directions *(no tape)*	8/	106/	9
identify valid public transport for tickets *(no tape)*	8/	106/	10
revise an itinerary from timetables *(no tape)*	9/	120/	11
note people's favorite seasons per dialogue	11/	139/	3
correct statements about preferences per dialogue	11/	139/	4
correct an apartment description per dialogue	13/	171/	6
decode script signatures *(no tape)*	13/	176/	10
correct mistakes in statements per letter in script	13/	176/	11
correct mistakes in people's plans per dialogue	14/	181/	1
find mismatches between dialogue statements and pictures	14/	187/	8
trace a route on a map per dialogue	15/	197/	1

Greek

Rearranging the Text

words from sentences in shopping dialogues	8/	114/	4
food order scrambled sentences from dialogue	10/	142/	3
scrambled answers on vacation plans *(tape confirms)*	15/	208/	3

True/False

food items available from dialogue	3/	44/	4

Multiple Choice

short getting-acquainted phrases from a dialogue	1/	15/	1
family relationships from dialogue	2/	30/	4
restaurant phrases from dialogue	3/	43/	1

food ordering and restaurant bill phrases | 3/ | 44/ | 3
locations of named places from dialogue | 4/ | 57/ | 2
money-changing scene to correspond with dialogue | 4/ | 58/ | 3
Greek translations of requests to repeat | 4/ | 58/ | 5
Greek words for bank, food, and hotel contexts *(no tape)* | 4/ | 60/ | Ex.
business hours of shops from dialogue | 6/ | 86/ | 4
colors as heard in phrase context on tape | 7/ | 100/ | 3
identify items on shopping list in Greek alphabet *(no tape)* | 8/ | 116/ | Ex.
responses to a taxi driver's question from tape prompts | 9/ | 128/ | 3
food item that doesn't belong with tape prompts | 10/ | 141/ | 1
answers to questions on future plans *(tape confirms)* | 15/ | 207/ | 1

Checking Off Items

restaurant order *(no tape)* | 3/ | 46/ | Ex.
numbers heard on tape from a list | 5/ | 72/ | 4
grocery items and weights from dialogue | 8/ | 114/ | 3
car service request from dialogue | 9/ | 127/ | 2
ingredients for a *horiátiki saláta (tape confirms)* | 10/ | 142/ | 4

Fill-Ins

getting-acquainted dialogue elements | 1/ | 16/ | 3
food items in restaurant ordering context | 3/ | 43/ | 2
prices of foods from dialogue | 3/ | 44/ | 5
hotel checking-in phrases from dialogue | 4/ | 57/ | 1
money amounts in money-changing context | 4/ | 58/ | 4
various words in a shopping dialogue | 7/ | 100/ | 4
words in a dialogue about food preferences | 11/ | 153/ | 2
countries matching capitals in Greek alphabet *(no tape)* | 11/ | 156/ | Ex.
personal facts from dialogue with visual clues | 12/ | 167/ | 1
personal fact dialogue, familiar and polite forms | 12/ | 168/ | 4
day's events from visual prompts *(tape confirms)* | 14/ | 195/ | 1
answer questions in future from prompts *(tape confirms)* | 15/ | 207/ | 2
select adjectives with appropriate endings | Rev./ | 217/ | 1

Grids

numbers 1-20 on "bingo" card	2/	30/	3
directions for named places from dialogue	5/	71/	1
hotel guest arrivals and departures from dialogue	6/	85/	1
hotel mealtimes from dialogue	6/	85/	1
ship timetable from dialogue	6/	85/	3
prices of groceries from dialogue	7/	99/	2
grocery items and prices from dialogue	8/	113/	1
travel details from dialogue	9/	127/	1
degrees of liking/disliking various things from dialogue	11/	153/	1
weather in European countries from a radio report	11/	154/	3
prices of cars from dialogue	Rev./	217/	2

Matchings

spoken personal information with pictures	1/	16/	4
	1/	16/	5
getting acquainted questions with answers	2/	29/	1
spoken job titles with pictures	2/	29/	2
requests for directions with answers *(tape confirms)*	5/	72/	3
sentences in a shopping dialogue *(tape confirms)*	7/	99/	1
sentences in a grocery-store dialogue	8/	113/	2
sentences in a car-rental dialogue *(tape confirms)*	9/	128/	4
food dishes with person ordering them from dialogue	10/	141/	2
personal fact sentences from dialogue	12/	167/	2
items in a telephone conversation	13/	181/	1
responses in past with questions *(tape confirms)*	14/	196/	3
elements in a dialogue getting directions	Rev./	216/	2

Translating

Greek place names used in directions *(no tape)*	5/	74/	Ex.
signage words *(no tape)*	7/	102/	Ex.
place names in Greek alphabet *(no tape)*	9/	130/	Ex.
ingredients for *mousaká* *(no tape)*	10/	144/	Ex.
country names in Greek alphabet *(no tape)*	12/	170/	Ex.
names of Greek letters *(tape confirms)*	13/	181/	2

88 Just Listen 'n Learn Language Programs

personal names in Greek alphabet	13/	182/	3
wares of various shops *(no tape)*	14/	198/	Rev.
hotel and restaurant words *(no tape)*	15/	210/	Rev.
personal food preference dialogue *(tape confirms)*	Rev./	219/	2
past and future events	Rev./	220/	1

Reenacting a Dialogue

simple conversation in beach context	Rev./	214/	4
respond with number and time phrases	Rev./	216/	3
practice phrases with *puo ine* and *pió sigá*	Rev./	216/	4
shopping and travel dialogue from tape prompts	Rev./	217/	3
ask personal questions from tape prompts	Rev./	219/	3
ask questions and use past and future	Rev./	220/	2

Miscellaneous

polite formulas crossword from tape prompts	1/	15/	2
trace directions on map and identify places	5/	71/	2
give time of day shown on clocks *(no tape)*	6/	87/	Ex.
replace familiar with polite forms *(tape confirms)*	12/	168/	3
fill in past tense verbs and translate	14/	196/	2
produce greeting suitable to stated situation	Rev./	213/	1
name pictured objects	Rev./	213/	2
practice writing Greek letters	Rev./	214/	3
common words crossword	Rev./	215/	1
write foods in correct menu sections *(tape confirms)*	Rev./	218/	1

Arabic

Dictation

names of people introduced	1/	11/	8

Rearranging the Text

repeat offers of drinks, changing gender	3/	37/	2
scrambled lines from an appointment dialogue	4/	55/	14
scrambled lines from a shopping dialogue	8/	111/	7
scrambled restaurant dialogue with waiter	10/	137/	8

scrambled story about a day's events	11/	153/	8
scrambled dialogue about a dinner invitation	14/	193/	4

True/False *(from dialogues)*

nationalities	1/	13/	10
appointments	4/	55/	10
locations of sites	5/	69/	7
working hours	6/	81/	7
prices of items	8/	113/	11
negotiations for a taxi trip	9/	121/	2
appointment made through an assistant	12/	163/	1
request to use a club's pool	13/	181/	6
arrangements for an evening out	14/	191/	2

Multiple Choice *(from dialogues)*

short personal information	2/	23/	1
café bill items	3/	39/	7
hotel room description	4/	51/	1
cost of a hotel room	4/	53/	7
appointment details	4/	55/	13
time of day	6/	79/	1
store hours	6/	81/	4
directions	7/	95/	5
grocery purchases	8/	107/	1
gift purchases	8/	109/	4
details on clothing purchases	8/	109/	5
details from an offer for a lift	9/	123/	8
food order	10/	135/	1
directions to a restaurant	10/	135/	2
food items ordered	10/	137/	7
food items from their descriptions	10/	139/	10
details from an office assistant's directions	12/	163/	2
details from an office visit	12/	165/	5
details about arranging to swim at a private pool	13/	181/	7
details about a speaker's plans for tonight	14/	191/	1

details about an invitation to a meal	14/	193/	5
details about summer plans	14/	195/	9
details about a recent trip	15/	209/	6

Checking Off Items

national identities of speakers	1/	9/	5
personal information about a speaker	2/	25/	4
phrases in Arabic from a simple conversation	2/	25/	5
menu items from a spoken list	3/	41/	9
time of day from a dialogue	6/	79/	2
items requested from a shopkeeper in a dialogue	7/	93/	2
items purchased in a dialogue	7/	99/	10
gifts purchased in a dialogue	8/	113/	10
information about renting a car from a dialogue	9/	125/	10
menu items from a dialogue	10/	137/	4
	10/	139/	9
someone's entertainment preferences from a dialogue	11/	149/	1
events in someone's trip from a dialogue	15/	205/	2

Fill-Ins

exchange greetings	1/	11/	7
speakers' personal information	1/	15/	12,13
personal reactions in a dialogue	2/	27/	7
getting acquainted dialogue elements	2/	29/	9
breakfast and coffee orders	3/	39/	5
room reservation dialogue elements	4/	53/	5
appointment dialogue elements	4/	55/	11
asking directions	5/	65/	2
service taxi route details	5/	67/	4
room locations in a building from a dialogue	5/	69/	8
dialogue elements for buying a newspaper	7/	93/	1
	7/	95/	4
dialogue elements for meeting a friend at a film	7/	97/	8
dialogue elements in shopping for a birthday present	8/	111/	8
dialogue elements at a gas station	9/	121/	5

words of liking and disliking in context	11/	149/	3
speaker's sport preferences from a dialogue	11/	151/	5
verbs and pronouns in a dialogue on horses	11/	151/	6
diary from a dialogue between a boss and a secretary	12/	165/	4
elements from a conversation to set up an appointment	12/	167/	7
diary from a dialogue between friends	12/	167/	8
dialogue elements from an invitation to lunch	14/	193/	7
verbs and phrases from a summary of a speaker's weekend	15/	207/	4
words and phrases in a dialogue about personal news	15/	209/	7

Grids

numbers 1–20 on a "bingo" card	2/	23/	2
items and their prices from a dialogue	3/	41/	10
sort personal information about two speakers from a dialogue	6/	83/	9
bus ticket information from a dialogue	7/	97/	7
transportation methods and costs from a dialogue	9/	127/	12

Matchings

getting acquainted dialogues with illustrations	1/	9/	2
getting acquainted dialogue elements with responses	1/	9/	4
food order dialogue answers with questions	3/	37/	1
restaurant items with English translation	3/	39/	4
spoken with written food orders	3/	41/	12
hotel room reservation requests	4/	51/	2
spoken with written room reservation	4/	53/	4
directions dialogue questions with answers	5/	65/	1
map keys with directions from a dialogue	5/	67/	5
shop supplies with prices	8/	107/	2
quantities with questions about a taxi trip	9/	121/	1
dialogue elements in interaction with a waiter	10/	137/	5
replies with tourist information questions and comments	13/	177/	1
people with their plans according to a dialogue	14/	195/	10
replies with dialogue questions about a trip to Egypt	15/	205/	1

Answering Informational Questions in English *(from dialogues)*

kinds of hotel rooms and their prices	4/	53/	8
working hours	6/	83/	10
details from a conversation with a bus station agent	9/	123/	7
details from a speaker's spoken reaction to a film	11/	155/	10
details about how to make a phone call	13/	177/	2
details about a visit to an amphitheater	13/	179/	4

Translating

ask bus route information	5/	71/	10

Answering Informational Questions in Arabic

getting-acquainted dialogue	1/	9/	3
personal questions	1/	13/	11
give directions to a taxi driver	1/	15/	14
short personal questions	2/	25/	6
short informal questions in a party context	2/	27/	8
give time of day from clock faces	6/	79/	3
respond with days of the week	6/	81/	8
questions about a trip to Syria	11/	153/	9

Reenacting a Dialogue

exchange simple greetings	1/	9/	6
greet a stranger and exchange names	1/	11/	9
exchange greetings and answer informational questions	2/	23/	3
ask for personal information	2/	29/	11
casual encounters at a café	3/	37/	3
breakfast orders at a café	3/	39/	6
ask a stranger if she speaks English	3/	39/	8
get a speaker to repeat or speak slowly	3/	41/	11
snack order at a café	3/	41/	13
hotel room reservations	4/	51/	3
reserve a room at a hotel	4/	53/	6
ask details about hotel rooms	4/	53/	9

arrange an appointment	4/	55/	12
	4/	55/	15
ask directions	5/	67/	3
clarify directions	5/	67/	6
reserve a hotel room and get directions	5/	69/	9
ask bus route information	5/	71/	11
answer questions about your working hours	6/	81/	6
answer questions about your work and residence	6/	83/	11
request items in a shop	7/	93/	3
say amounts of Jordanian money	7/	95/	6
purchase postcards from a shopkeeper	7/	97/	9
purchase tickets to a film	7/	99/	11
purchase a gift at a shop	8/	107/	3
	8/	109/	6
purchase an embroidered blouse	8/	111/	9
browsing in a gift shop	8/	113/	12
negotiate a taxi trip	9/	121/	3
discuss a bus trip with a driver	9/	121/	6
ask for information at a bus station	9/	123/	9
rent a car	9/	125/	11
get information about hors d'œuvres at a restaurant	10/	135/	3
explain menu selections to a friend and ask preferences	10/	137/	6
order a complete meal at a restaurant	10/	139/	11
express food preferences	11/	149/	2
express reactions to Jordan	11/	149/	4
express dissatisfactions with a hotel	11/	155/	11
arrange an appointment with a receptionist	12/	163/	3
make a business appointment	12/	165/	6
arrange and accept a dinner invitation	12/	167/	9
get information on making international phone calls	13/	177/	3
get information on making a local phone call	13/	179/	5
get information on using a hotel pool	13/	181/	8
invite a friend out	14/	191/	3
respond to an invitation from an acquaintance	14/	191/	6

invite a friend to dinner 14/ 193/ 8
respond in a social encounter with a stranger 15/ 205/ 3
recount events from a vacation in Amman 15/ 207/ 5

Miscellaneous

identify masculine and feminine inflections 1/ 9/ 1
read numbers 1–20 2/ 29/ 10
repeat days of the week 6/ 81/ 5
extract details from a dialogue on finding a gas station 9/ 121/ 4
give formulaic responses to various greetings 9/ 127/ 13
extract details from a dialogue about a trip 11/ 153/ 7

Notes

Notes

Notes

FOREIGN LANGUAGE BOOKS

Multilingual
The Insult Dictionary:
　How to Give 'Em Hell in 5 Nasty
　Languages
The Lover's Dictionary:
　How to be Amorous in 5 Delectable
　Languages
Multilingual Phrase Book
Let's Drive Europe Phrasebook
CD-ROM "Languages of the World":
　Multilingual Dictionary Database

Spanish
Vox Spanish and English Dictionaries
NTC's Dictionary of Spanish False Cognates
Nice 'n Easy Spanish Grammar
Spanish Verbs and Essentials of Grammar
Getting Started in Spanish
Spanish à la Cartoon
Guide to Spanish Idioms
Guide to Correspondence in Spanish
The Hispanic Way

French
NTC's New College French and English
　Dictionary
French Verbs and Essentials of Grammar
Real French
Getting Started in French
Guide to French Idioms
Guide to Correspondence in French
French à la Cartoon
Nice 'n Easy French Grammar
NTC's Dictionary of *Faux Amis*
NTC's Dictionary of Canadian French
Au courant: Expressions for Communicating in
　Everyday French

German
Schöffler-Weis German and English Dictionary
Klett German and English Dictionary
Getting Started in German
German Verbs and Essentials of Grammar
Guide to German Idioms
Street-wise German
Nice 'n Easy German Grammar
German à la Cartoon
NTC's Dictionary of German False Cognates

Italian
Zanichelli Super-Mini Italian and English
　Dictionary
Zanichelli New College Italian and English
　Dictionary
Getting Started in Italian
Italian Verbs and Essentials of Grammar

Greek
NTC's New College Greek and English
　Dictionary

Latin
Essentials of Latin Grammar

Hebrew
Everyday Hebrew

Chinese
Easy Chinese Phrasebook and Dictionary

Korean
Korean in Plain English

Polish
The Wiedza Powszechna Compact Polish and
　English Dictionary

Swedish
Swedish Verbs and Essentials of Grammar

Russian
Complete Handbook of Russian Verbs
Essentials of Russian Grammar
Business Russian
Basic Structure Practice in Russian

Japanese
Easy Kana Workbook
Easy Hiragana
Easy Katakana
101 Japanese Idioms
Japanese in Plain English
Everyday Japanese
Japanese for Children
Japanese Cultural Encounters
Nissan's Business Japanese

"Just Enough" Phrase Books
Chinese, Dutch, French, German, Greek,
　Hebrew, Hungarian, Italian, Japanese,
　Portuguese, Russian, Scandinavian,
　Serbo-Croat, Spanish
Business French, Business German, Business
　Spanish

Audio and Video Language Programs
Just Listen 'n Learn Spanish, French,
　German, Italian, Greek, and Arabic
Just Listen 'n Learn...Spanish,
　French, German PLUS
Conversational...Spanish, French, German,
　Italian, Russian, Greek, Japanese, Thai,
　Portuguese in 7 Days
Practice & Improve Your...Spanish, French,
　Italian, and German
Practice & Improve Your...Spanish, French,
　Italian, and German PLUS
Improve Your...Spanish, French, Italian, and
　German: The P&I Method
VideoPassport French
VideoPassport Spanish
How to Pronounce...Spanish, French,
　German, Italian, Russian, Japanese
　Correctly

PASSPORT BOOKS
a division of *NTC Publishing Group*
Lincolnwood, Illinois USA